Sharon R. Sakson

Brussels Griffons

Everything About Purchase, Care, Nutrition, Behavior, and Training

Filled with Full-color Photographs

Illustrations by Pam Tanzey

BARRON'S

CONTENTS

LS

INTRODUCING THE BRUSSELS GRIFFON

The Brussels Griffon is a captivating toy dog, intelligent, alert, sensitive, and full of self-importance. He has a round face with big eyes and an almost human expression. He is happy and confident, convinced that he deserves to be the center of attention. He is devoted to his owner but is always willing to make new friends.

Description

The Brussels Griffon is the monkey-faced imp of the toy breeds. He is a lively, sturdy little fellow. As owners of this breed know, he may be small, but his personality is big. He moves confidently, with his ears and tail alert. His eyes are large and bright, his chin is upturned, and he charms his friends with a countenance that can seem human at times.

Brussels Griffons are wonderful companions—loving, healthy, smart, and eager to please. They are happy to go wherever their owner goes. If you love them, they return that investment a hundredfold.

They have long been popular as pets in Europe, whereas in the United States they were rare for many years, ranking around #98 in the American Kennel Club's list of most popular breeds. But the breed has since gained favor, climbing to #50 on the list. The popularity is well-deserved, as these dogs make excellent family pets.

Coat: Brussels Griffons come in two coats, rough and smooth. The rough-coated dog is by far the more popular. He grows a bushy beard, which adds to his enchanting expression. There is a wide variation in texture of the rough coats. Some have the extremely hard or wiry coat similar to that of terrier breeds, while others have a softer, fluffy coat, with more coat types filling the entire spectrum in between.

The rough coat does not shed. It continues to grow, which means the dog needs grooming every two months or so to keep him looking neat and feeling comfortable. Because Griffs with this type of coat don't shed, people who are usually allergic to dogs are often not allergic to Brussels Griffons.

Dog show exhibitors prize long and full "furnishings"—the hair on the legs. Dogs with

Smooth coat (left)
Rough coat (right)

The AKC Standard calls for a coat that is "wiry and dense, the harder and more wiry the better." If the coat is truly hard and wiry, the beard and furnishings tend to be sparse, because hard hair breaks

plush beards and other such ornamental features look flashy in the show ring, but it is difficult to keep long furnishings on a house dog, because the hair breaks when the dog plays and rolls around.

before it grows very long. The advantage of the hard, wiry coat is that it requires less grooming. Griffons who have one rough parent and one smooth parent tend to have the hardest coats. Rough coats are hand stripped for the show ring. At home, most people use clippers to keep their dogs' coats neat.

Elijah's Story

Elijah began his show life as a natural-eared dog. He had beautiful conformation and movement but failed to win any points. Each judge told his owner, Bertie, that Elijah was a quality dog, but they couldn't reward him because of his uncropped ears. In frustration, she took him, at age three, to a veterinarian who performed the cropping operation. With his new, neater appearance, he quickly won his championship.

A standard of perfection: The breed standard is a written document put together by the national breed club that fully describes what the perfect Brussels Griffon would look like. It is a blueprint for breeders so that they can choose sires and dams who most closely fit the description. At shows, dogs are judged on how closely they conform to the standard. The Brussels Griffon standard can be found on the AKC Web site.

The big advantage to smooth coats is that they are wash-and-wear and don't require any stripping or clipping at all. On the other hand, smooth-coated Griffs do shed, though not as much as Pugs. There is some variation in smooth coats; some are sleek, tight, and glossy, like the Boston Terrier, while others are thicker and softer, like the Smooth Fox Terrier.

Colors: There are four recognized colors of Brussels Griffons: red, belge, black and tan, and black. The red variety is reddish brown, with a little black at the whiskers and chin allowable. This color ranges from a deep mahogany through a fiery red. In the show ring, light fawn, blond, or tan is not desirable. Belge is black and reddish brown mixed, usually with black mask and whiskers. "Belge" is called "wild boar" on a Wirehaired Dachshund. This color is rare. However, inexperienced breeders often mark their puppies' colors as "belge" because they don't realize that the black coat most puppies have at birth will disappear in a few weeks to become red. Black and tan Griffons are jet black with rich deep tan points. The black and tan is the same color and pattern as seen on a Doberman Pinscher. Black dogs are solid black. Some black roughs have grayish or tan undercoats.

Natural or cropped ears? Brussels Griffons' ears should be small, in keeping with their sweet, quirky faces. Natural Brussels Griffon ears are semi-erect, while most Griffs in the show ring have had their ears cropped to a small, erect triangle.

Originally, owners cropped their dogs' ears for several reasons. For one, they believed it allowed their dogs to hear better. However, experiments have shown that this is not true; dogs hear just as well no matter what kind of ears they have. A second purpose was to prevent infection, as the dropped ear flap creates a dark, moist canal, a perfect environment for such problems. (You will often see dogs with long drop ears, such as Spaniels, shaking their heads from side to side and scratching, trying to clear an itch.) A third reason was to eliminate soft folds of skin that could be grabbed by a rat or other vermin during the hunt.

Cropping today is done only for cosmetic purposes. It requires surgery by a veterinarian to remove a portion of the ear flap.

Show exhibitors often prefer the cropped ears because they look alert and active, whereas natural ears can look sloppy. The Standard asks for small ears. Cropped ears can be shaped to the small size; natural ears might be larger. Show judges tend to lean toward the dog with cropped ears.

Cropping has been banned in England and all other European countries as well as in Australia for reasons of cruelty. There is a definite trend

Natural ears (left)
Cropped ears (right)

among show breeders in the United States and Canada to leave Brussels Griffons' ears natural.

Temperament

Griffs love games and have a sense of humor. They need to be close to their people to be happy. They need to be devoted to someone. Griffs become depressed if left alone, without attention. On the flip side, this devotion creates dependency on the owner that not everyone is prepared to handle.

Griffons make excellent pets for single people or empty-nesters who need a companion, as well as for busy families. They like to be with you and do what you do. They like to take walks and explore, but they're perfectly content to sit with you and watch TV or observe as you make dinner. They're happy as long as they're with you. They like to be held. They like to be right up close on your lap or right next to you in the chair, or on the floor by your feet. Owning a Griff is like having a baby around, a small dependent toddler who never grows up. As one breeder put it, "Brussels Griffons are not dogs. They are little people."

Griffons love to play.

History

Brussels Griffons are named for the city of their origin, Brussels, in Belgium. During the early 1800s the breed was more or less adopted by stable boys and coachmen to keep rats away. The dogs were great at that job but also proved to be such good companions that their owners took them everywhere. Griffons soon attracted the attention of women who wanted a small, intelligent family dog. Even royalty took notice of the wonderful breed. Queen Astrid of Belgium became a Brussels Griffon owner in 1894, breeding and exhibiting her dogs in the new sport of dog shows.

In the mid-1800s the American artist Mary Cassatt kept several at her home in Paris and depicted a black and tan Brussels Griffon in her painting *Susan on a Balcony Holding a Dog* (c. 1882); about a decade earlier, in 1870, the French Impressionist Pierre-Auguste Renoir painted *La Baigneuse au Griffon (The Bather with a Griffon)*.

The early specimens were the result of crossings of the Affenpinscher, Miniature Pinscher, Dutch Smoushond, and small terrier-type breeds that are now extinct. At the time the breed emerged from the stables of Belgium, two notable crosses were made that permanently affected the look of the Brussels Griffon: one to the solid-red-colored Ruby King Charles Spaniel, and the other to the black Pug.

From the Ruby Spaniel the Griffon acquired the distinctive rounded head, upturned jaw, and rich red color, while from the Pug a smooth-

Brussels Griffons are alert and outgoing.

The Petit Brabançon.

haired version of the Griff was created. The smooth version is known in Europe as the Petit Brabançon, which cannot be interbred with the rough-coated type without formal kennel club permission. Because the smooths are like the roughs in every point except coat, the English-speaking countries decided to include both under one breed name, and they are interbred. The Pug also contributed the color black to the three colors already known in the breed: red, black and tan, and belge (black and reddish brown).

Before those crosses, the Brussels Griffon had a spaniel-like muzzle with a strong jaw and punishing teeth, elements he needed to do his work as a ratter. The crosses forever changed the Brussels Griffon to a brachycephalic breed—that is, having a round head with a shortened muzzle. The Ruby Spaniel and Pug are largely responsible for the facial characteristics that are so much a part of the present-day Griff,

Petit Brabancon

The Petit Brabançon, or smooth-coated Brussels Griffon, gets its name from the national anthem of Belgium, *La Brabançonne (The Song of Brabant)*. Brabant is a province of central Belgium.

whose very short, uptilted nose and upswept jaw now make it impossible for him to catch vermin, work to which he was once well suited. But the Griff has a new job now, one he performs very well: as an intriguing, alert, and devoted companion.

Griffons arrived in the United States in the 1890s. The breed entered the AKC stud book in 1899 and exhibitors presented them at the Westminster Kennel Club show the same year. They received official American Kennel Club (AKC) recognition in 1900.

With their outgoing attitude and confident appearance, Brussels Griffons often do well in the show ring, winning Group placements and Best in Shows. One of the first champions to call attention to the breed in the Group ring was Champion Barmere's Mighty Man, who exemplified the breed's small but powerful presence. Griffs also do well in Obedience and Agility competitions, because they are intelligent, usually easily motivated by food, and athletic enough for jumps and tunnels.

What's in a name? Newcomers to the Brussels Griffon breed often shorten the name to "Brussels," but this is not correct. German Shepherds are not called "Germans," nor are English Setters called "English." The correct term is "Griffon," or the nickname "Griff" or "Griffy." Brussels is the capital of Belgium. A griffon (or gryphon) is a mythical animal with the head and wings of an eagle, erect ears, and the body, hind legs, and tail of a lion. Griffon figures are often seen on medieval cathedrals in European cities, where they function as gargoyles to ward off evil spirits.

The Brachycephalic Dog: Dogs With Pushed-In Faces

The word comes from the Greek roots *brachy,* meaning short, and *kephalé,* meaning head. Brachycephalic dogs have a normal lower jaw in proportion to their body size and a compressed upper jaw. Brussels Griffons are brachycephalic but are not as prone to some of the health problems that may afflict other breeds in this category, which include:

- Boxer
- Pug
- Pekingese
- Japanese Chin
- Boston Terrier
- Bulldog
- French Bulldog

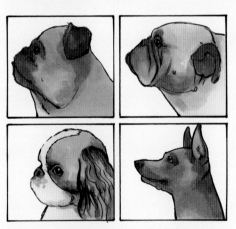

The Pug, Bulldog, and English Toy Spaniel are all brachycephalic breeds. In contrast, the Miniature Pinscher has the "wolf-like" muzzle.

GETTING A BRUSSELS GRIFFON

Griffons are smart, lovable, funny, eager to please and generally easy to train. Nonetheless, do your homework to make sure this breed is suited to your family and lifestyle.

Is the Brussels Griffon for You?

The Brussels Griffon is primarily a quiet fellow. He is not given to lots of yappy barking at random sounds, as some toy breeds are. He should not be hired as a guard dog, as he is not big enough and tends to like everybody who comes into the house. Brussels Griffons don't seem to realize that they weigh only 8 to 12 pounds (3.6 to 5.4 kg), and usually will stand up to much bigger dogs.

Their health is generally very good. The rough coats do not shed, but the coat grows quickly and requires clipping every two months or so. Smooths shed, but not a lot. The long beard of the roughs gets dirty easily and has to be brushed or cleaned often to get out food and other debris. After they drink from their bowl, the roughs often trail droplets of water across the kitchen floor.

Reputable breeders usually will question you about your lifestyle and why you want a Brussels Griffon. Most everyone works, so it is normal for dogs to be alone eight hours a day. But for people who have numerous hobbies or commitments that require them to spend a lot of time away from home, a Brussels Griffon would not be a good choice. These dogs love human company and become depressed if left alone too long, And, even though they are small, they need exercise in order to thrive. They need the discipline of a caring owner, as well as affection, which they will return in huge quantities.

The Brussels Griffon has never been a really popular breed, like Golden Retrievers or Dachshunds. It used to be that few people recognized the breed. But that changed after the release of the movie *As Good as It Gets* in 1997, which featured a Griffon named Verdell,

Brussels Griffons do not need a large backyard.

who displayed all the funny and loving traits of the breed, charming and entertaining his owner and the next-door neighbor played by Jack Nicholson.

That film brought popularity to the breed and led a lot of people to acquire Brussels Griffons because they thought Verdell was cute. The breed *is* cute, but Griffs require the same attention, care, and training as any dog, including housebreaking, leash training, grooming, and socializing. They are not wind-up toys. They require a lot of time, so be honest with yourself about how much time and work you are willing and able to devote to raising a dog properly. Many Brussels Griffons are turned into shelters or rescue centers when people realize that they are not stuffed toys and have the same needs as any larger dog.

Size: The great thing about Brussels Griffons is that they are small and cooperative. They don't need a large backyard in which to roam

and they are wonderful pets for apartment dwellers because they don't take up much room and love to walk the city streets.

For people who are able to take their pet with them to work, the Griffon is perfect because of his small size and cooperative nature. Griffons can be carried easily in their owner's arms or in pet carriers. They are usually easy to crate train and will sleep or rest happily and quietly near their owners.

Children: If they are well socialized, Brussels Griffons are great with children and seem to understand that children aren't always gentle, and are forgiving of tugs on their beards and tails. However, because Griffs weigh so little and are only about 14 inches (35.6 cm) high, they need to be protected from being dropped or roughly treated, even by well-intentioned children who simply want to play. How your Brussels Griffon gets along with children depends on you. Children who want to pet a dog are often over-eager and rush into the dog's face. It is up to you to show them how to gently stroke from the neck across the back—never on the head, as it is small and the eyes could easily be poked or the nostrils blocked. Teach children that it is best to stroke all animals from behind the ears. That is a much less confrontational approach.

The best way for a child to hold a Griff is to sit down on the floor and take the dog onto his or her lap. Griffon puppies are usually squirming with happiness and can easily slip out of a child's arms. If the child is sitting on the floor, the puppy cannot be dropped.

Show your older children how to scoop up the puppy and hold him firmly against their chest. Never let them pick up the puppy by his legs. And, of course, Griffon ears are not for pulling.

Parents with young children might look for an older dog that has had some training. However, if selecting a puppy, it's a good idea to let the child sit on the floor and see which puppy chooses him. Animals sometimes have an uncanny knack of knowing whom they belong with.

Once you get home, let the child and puppy play, carefully watching that the play does not get too rough. You may have to explain to your child that the puppy is a baby and that you need to be gentle with it. The best way for children and Griffons to interact is to give the child a small, soft toy that can be used to gently play tug of war or thrown for the puppy to run after. Or let the child give the puppy a small dog biscuit.

Will my child be allergic? Brussels Griffons are among those breeds classified as hypoallergenic, meaning that they have a relatively low capacity to induce allergic reactions. No breed

Griffs are great with kids.

is totally nonallergenic. Allergic people generally tolerate Brussels Griffons very easily because these dogs don't shed and have a low level of dander, particularly as compared to Sporting, Hound, or Working breeds. A recent medical study showed that children who grew up in a home with pets did not develop allergies to animals, probably because their immune systems learned how to handle the potential stressors of pet hair and dander. But the only way to know for sure is through trial and error. It would be helpful if you could visit someone who owns a Griffon and note your child's allergic reaction.

Finding a Brussels Griffon

Now that you've decided that Brussels Griffons are the right breed for you, how do you find one?

Dog publications—from the library, pet store, or magazine rack—have ads from breeders. The Internet has turned out to be a great boon to people searching for a puppy. You can check the Web sites of the Brussels Griffon clubs for lists of breeders.

Buy your dog from a reputable, responsible breeder. See for yourself that the Brussels Griffons being bred have good temperament and health. Choose a breeder who's experienced and willing to guide and advise you about care and training throughout the dog's life.

Good breeders will ask about your history with dogs and if your schedule allows you enough time to care for a puppy. They know all about the health and temperament of the parents, and their correct weight, and have photos, pedigrees, and health records of their dogs. Reputable breeders keep their dogs clean and

Important Questions to Ask the Breeder

- How old are the pups?
- Which sex is available?
- Have they had their shots?
- Did they get a health check from a veterinarian?
- Is the litter AKC registered?
- Were the pups handled and socialized frequently?
- What kind of food are they eating?

Ask to see the parents, littermates, or any family members of the puppies, to get an idea what the puppies will be like when they're grown.

Ask for a 72-hour money-back guarantee to take the puppy to your veterinarian. (Most states have "Puppy Lemon Laws" that make sellers responsible for sick puppies.)

groomed and raise their puppies in the house, in a location where they can keep a close eye on them, and where the puppies can be handled frequently. They guarantee that the puppy's health is good, and will take the puppy back if he does not pass a veterinarian check. They should be available to you throughout the dog's life with any questions you have.

Once you find a reputable breeder, if they don't have puppies immediately available, ask to be placed on the waiting list. Brussels Griffons have small litters. Litters of one, two or three puppies are common. It can be hard to find a puppy in the time frame you have in mind.

While visiting the breeder, be sure to ask questions. Take a list with you. There are many things you can learn from the breeder about how to

Search for just the right puppy.

Some Questions a Breeder Might Ask

- Have you ever had a Brussels Griffon before?
- Why do you want one?
- Have you cared for a dog before?
- What happened to your last dog?
- What would the puppy's life be like with you?
- If you are gone more than about eight hours a day, will someone else be there to take care of the dog?
- Is this puppy planned to be a surprise gift? Most breeders will not let a puppy go in that case. They want to know that the new owner really wants the dog and is prepared to take on the responsibility of training and caring for him.

care for and train your puppy. Good breeders want to make sure their puppies go to good homes, with people who know what to expect and have made all the necessary preparations.

The breeder will provide a bill of sale, the puppy's health record, registration papers, and the terms of his or her guarantee. You will want to take the puppy to your own veterinarian as soon as possible to make sure he's healthy and get started on the inoculation schedule that your veterinarian recommends.

Male or Female?

New buyers always want to know which sex will make the best pet. The truth is, they both will. For people who are not planning to breed, neutering the male or spaying the female Griff will alleviate a lot of problems, like "marking" territory and humping other dogs.

Many breeders feel that, as pets, the females are slightly more independent-minded and the males slightly more loving. As a practical matter, if you had two Griffs in the yard, a male and a female, and you called them to come to you, the male would run to you as fast as he could, and the female would look up as if to say, "Just a minute!" As to which you should buy, it's a matter of personal preference.

Puppy or Adult?

Puppies are cute, cuddly, and fun, but they are also lots of work. Puppies demand a lot of time for their housebreaking and training. Nonetheless, raising a puppy is a rewarding experience, as you see him through all the stages of his life.

Older dogs are usually more settled. They don't need as much exercise and attention and have passed through the chewing stage. They may have had some type of training, formal or informal. Older dogs are often better with children because they are less demanding.

Adults from breeders: It's rare that a breeder has an older dog for sale, but sometimes show exhibitors have a dog they want to retire from the show ring.

Adults from rescue: Other sources of an older dog are a shelter or rescue program. The National Brussels Griffon Club runs a wonderful rescue program; on its Web site you will find photos of available dogs, along with their location and a little bit about them.

Rescue dogs are often a good choice for someone who doesn't want the hassle of a little puppy. When a dog enters a rescue program, he is evaluated using the information received from the owner, the foster home, and/or the shelter personnel. Rescue volunteers have the

Puppies are born with dark coats that turn to red after the first clipping or handstripping.

dog checked by a veterinarian, so he's healthy when he goes to a new home. They also try to get a sense of the Griffon's temperament and how he gets along with people, children, cats, and other dogs. Then they try to match up the Griffon with the best possible home.

The most common reasons Griffons are turned in to rescue are job transfers, owner's death, divorce, moving to an apartment that does not allow dogs, or someone in the family is allergic. But across the nation, the number-one reason a dog is turned into a shelter is the owner's inability to housebreak him. This problem is the fault of the owner, not the dog.

Some dogs turned in to rescue have been mistreated or abandoned. If that's the case, the Griffon may need extra love and care to convince him that he has found a loving home where he'll be safe. But overwhelmingly, Griffons adopted from rescue are wonderful little pets, loving and sensitive, willing to please. They only need a chance and time to become beloved companions in your home.

Puppy Paperwork
The breeder should supply you with:
✔ A record of the puppy's shots
✔ A health certificate from a veterinarian
✔ A registration for the AKC
✔ A pedigree

Show or Pet
Show breeders are always looking for their next champion. If you think you would like to become involved in the sport of showing dogs,

Adults make great pets. They get along well with other dogs.

tell that to the breeder, who can guide you to the puppy with the best head, best movement, correct expression, correct coat. Breeders usually charge a premium price for their show-quality puppies.

If you want a Griffon to love and enjoy and don't plan on showing him in the conformation ring, you want the one whose personality is most appealing to you. Both the show puppies and pet puppies should share completely the same good health and happy temperament.

How Big, How Small?

The written Standard for Brussels Griffons says that their weight should be from 8 to 10 pounds (3.6 to 4.5 kg), but should not exceed 12 pounds (5.4 kg). Sometimes, a litter of normal size parents will contain a tiny one who

grows to only 6 or 7 pounds (2.7 or 3.2 kg). This is because different breeds were used in the creation of the Brussels Griffon, and some were smaller, such as the Yorkshire Terrier. Since the genetic material for smaller ones is in the breed, they sometimes pop up.

There were many smaller ones in the early 1900s, as is apparent from photos of the time, and we can see from the written record of dog shows that classes were adjusted to add some specifically for the smaller Griffs. There were also some larger breeds in the Griffon's background, like the Smoushond. And every once in a while, a larger Griff shows up. But those smaller and larger ones should not be bred.

Find out the weight of your puppy's parents. That's the best way to gauge how big the offspring will be. If a breeder is using dams that

Registration Statistics of Brussels Griffons

For most of the last century, the Brussels Griffon's ranking among registered breeds was very low, #96 out of more than 125 breeds. In 1997, the year the movie *As Good as It Gets* came out, his ranking started to rise, to #91 in 1997 and to #60 in 2005.

Over the course of ten years, Brussels Griffon registrations increased by 231 percent! Only Cavalier King Charles Spaniels and French Bulldogs grew faster in numbers of dogs registered.

At present, approximately 1,800 Brussels Griffons are registered every year.

are larger than 12 pounds (5.4 kg), it is probably in an attempt to get more puppies and to avoid delivering by Cesarean section. But even if the large ones are nice dogs, they are not true Brussels Griffons.

AKC Registration

The American Kennel Club is the oldest, largest, and most prestigious of the dog clubs in the United States. It is made up of 5,000 member clubs, all of which hold dog shows, obedience trials, agility trials, and various other tests in which AKC-registered Brussels Griffons may take part. The AKC requires that breeders submit DNA samples from their frequently used breeding stock. This is used to guarantee that a puppy is who the breeder says he is.

If the parentage of a Brussels Griffon cannot be proven through DNA testing, he cannot be AKC registered. If a breeder is raising Brussels Griffons that are not AKC registered, one reason might be that their parentage is in question.

Because the AKC is so strict, other registries have cropped up. Some of these will grant registration papers to Brussels Griffons without proof of their breeding, which means it is possible for an unscrupulous person to cross a Brussels Griffon to another breed, such as a Pug or a Yorkshire Terrier, or any other breed, and still be able to get papers calling it a Brussels Griffon. These puppies might be cute, but they are not true Brussels Griffons.

The important thing to realize is that only AKC-registered Brussels Griffons can compete in AKC events. When you ask the breeder about registration, make sure you get a clear answer as to which registry she used. It does make a difference.

Selecting a Puppy

Because Brussels Griffon litters are so small, new owners don't usually get a chance to pick from among many puppies. Even so, don't rush. Take your time to watch the puppy play and see how he interacts with you. It's easy to fall in love with adorable baby puppies. But this is going to be a new member of your family who will be with you for many years. Dog ownership is a long-term commitment.

Here are some things for you to evaluate when looking for a potential new family member.

General attitude: The puppy should be alert, happy, and active. If he races about, plays hard, and is a little imp, he is probably in good health. A listless puppy is not a good sign.

Puppies have very delineated cycles to their day. They play hard, and then they sleep. Puppies love to meet new people. But after playing for awhile, they collapse into sleep again. A puppy who mopes about, with little energy,

Healthy puppies are alert and active.

may be sick. Pick another puppy, or come back on another day to see if he acts differently.

Soundness: As the puppy plays, check to make sure he does not limp or favor one leg. Watch him travel across the floor. A dog who sometimes shakes or stretches his rear leg while exercising may have a potential problem with subluxating patellas. The puppy who can run, jump, dive, leap, and pull on a toy with no problems is a sound puppy.

Breathing: Hold the puppy and look directly in his face. The nostrils should be well opened for easy breathing. Narrow nostrils are a problem. Normal Brussels Griffon puppies don't make a lot of breathing sounds. Heavy snuffling may be a sign of kennel cough or another problem.

Heavy breathing sounds in a puppy will only get worse as he matures into adulthood.

Above all, he should not cough. Kennel cough is usually not serious in an adult, but it can be dangerous to tiny puppies and can easily turn

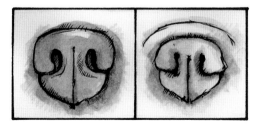

Normal nostrils (left)
Narrow or closed nostril (right)

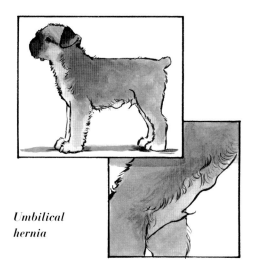

Umbilical hernia

into pneumonia. A puppy with a cough will usually need two or three weeks to get over it, and he'll need antibiotics.

Stool: You don't always get a chance to see the puppy's stool, but if he does eliminate, the stool should be firm and well formed. A loose stool is a sign of worms or intestinal infection. These are common puppy conditions and not serious, but they should be cleared up before he goes to a new home. If the stool is loose after the dog has received medication, it is a sign of a more serious problem.

Skin: The puppy should have smooth, unblemished skin. If he scratches, pick him up and check that spot. Red spots or dry patches could be anything from fleas to a skin allergy to ringworm.

Eyes: Eyes should be open and clear. There should not be any pus or discharge. However, baby puppies in this breed often have runny eyes and runny noses. This is most noticeable during the teething stage. They grow out of this tendency at about ten months. If the eyes or

nose are watery, check the puppy's body temperature, which should be cool and never feel hot to the touch. If he does feel warm, hopefully the breeder or kennel owner will take his temperature to see if he's sick.

Veterinarian Health Check

The veterinarian checks the puppy's temperature rectally. He holds the puppy, making sure he's normally active and not limp or lethargic.

He checks for hernias. If the hole where the umbilical cord was attached doesn't close all the way, a hernia forms. (This is a bit like a bellybutton that's "out.") Most are small and not serious. The veterinarian determines if the hernia penetrates the abdomen wall and needs to be repaired by surgery. The other type of hernia is inguinal, and shows up as a slight swelling on either side of the abdomen. It's rare.

The veterinarian goes over the body, searching for fleas, ticks, and any skin irritations. He *gently* manipulates the patellas (kneecaps) to make sure they are in place; they are not attached to the bone but are secured by muscles and ligaments. Normal patellas can be disjointed by strong manipulation, so handling of the patellas should always be gentle.

On the skull, he checks to see if there is a "soft spot," or fontanelle. A fontanelle is formed when the bone of the skull does not fully cover the brain. Chihuahua puppies nearly always have fontanelles, and they occur occasionally in Brussels Griffon puppies. If so, the spot should be very small. It will close as the puppy grows. But until it closes, the puppy can be badly injured by any kind of blow to the head, because the brain is not protected. So you need to know if there is a fontanelle present.

The veterinarian checks the puppy's face to make sure his nostrils are open, he's breathing normally, and his eyes are clear and not red or inflamed. He'll look in the mouth to check for gums that are pink, not gray, and normal baby teeth.

He uses an otoscope to probe the ear canal. With a stethoscope, he listens to the heart and lungs. A stool sample is checked for worms.

Ask questions to make sure you have a complete picture of your puppy's health.

Related Breeds— Affenpinschers and Pugs

Potential dog owners who are considering a Brussels Griffon are often equally drawn to the Affenpinscher, an older breed that was used in the creation of the Brussels Griffon. The two breeds are the same size, with similar coats of a harsh, wiry texture that need to be hand stripped for the show ring. Brussels Griffons usually come in red; Affenpinschers usually come in black. The strongest physical difference is in the head: the Affen is not brachycephalic—he does not have the "pushed in" face.

The two breeds are different in temperament. Brussels Griffons are friendly and outgoing. They love their families, but are quite willing to be friends with everybody else. Affenpinschers are more reserved. They are devoted to their own families but tend to hold back their opinion of new people and won't approach them until convinced that they are worthy of attention. These dogs can be stubborn; they are busy, bright, and pushy, as well as loving and protective. A woman who has been involved with both breeds says that if you turn a Brussels Griffon up ten notches, that's an Affenpinscher.

Why Are Brussels Griffons So Expensive?

The price reflects the expense of whelping and raising a litter. Like most toy breeds, Brussels Griffons often have trouble delivering their puppies. Puppies become stuck in the uterus, or are too big to come out naturally. So the bitch needs a Cesarean section operation, usually in the middle of the night at an emergency hospital that is even more expensive than the regular veterinarian.

Griffon puppies are fragile in their early weeks because they are so tiny. They require a lot of special care and attention, and sometimes, veterinarian visits. Dewclaws have to be removed. Puppy mortality is high. Statistics show that in the toy breeds, the puppy mortality rate is about fifty percent.

The litters are small. Litters of one, two, or three are usual. This makes the breeders' investment per puppy higher than in breeds used to whelping six to eight puppies.

People who like Brussels Griffons also tend to like Pugs. Both are brachycephalic. Early Brussels Griffons had long muzzles; the current round head was created by crossing to the Ruby English Toy Spaniel, which was itself created by crossing a Toy Spaniel to a Pug. There were also direct crosses to Pugs. Pugs should weigh from 14 to 18 pounds (6.4 to 8.2 kg); while Brussels Griffons are smaller, at 8 to 12 pounds (3.2 to 5.4 kg). Brussels Griffons as a breed have fewer health problems than Pugs. Pugs have extremely thick, short coats that shed. Brussels Griffons with rough coats do not shed; smooths shed, but not as much as Pugs. The Griff probably got much of his extremely loving personality from the Pug.

LIVING WITH A BRUSSELS GRIFFON

Brussels Griffons charm us with their clever personalities, almost human expressions, and intelligence. In return, they have some special needs that require extra knowledge on the part of their owners. In time and with loving attention, they become great companions and valued members of the household.

Bringing Your New Dog Home

One reason breeders strongly urge new owners not to buy a dog as an impulse purchase is that there are so many things to prepare for. When you bring the dog home to a house where nothing is ready, and you haven't thought about where she is going to spend her time, where her eating and playing and sleeping areas are going to be, and you're just winging it, confusion results. Things may not work out well. That sometimes leads to so much stress that the dog is sent off to the pound.

In the best of scenarios, you've given a lot of thought to caring for your new dog. You've purchased the items you'll need. You should have papers down where you want the puppy to pee. Have her bowls and bed in place. Start right from the beginning by introducing her to her area. She doesn't get to wander all over the house, because with a lot of territory to explore, a dog can easily become a housebreaking problem. Keep her confined, or keep her close to you.

Shopping for the Essentials

Collar: The best collar for a puppy is a soft nylon in a small size, 7 to 8 inches (18 to 20 cm), but leather and rolled leather collars work equally well. Don't use a chain collar. Look for one that is easily adjustable so that as she grows, you can keep letting it out. You should take it off every two weeks to a month to make it slightly larger. Collars for adult Griffons need to be sized very carefully so that they will not slip off over the head if she pulls on her leash. The size is correct if it allows you to slip your fingers under it but is not so loose that you can pull it off.

Puppy Proofing Your Home

- Have a barrier to keep your puppy in one room, usually the kitchen, so she can't wander the house.
- Check that doors close securely so she can't get outside.
- Keep cabinets with cleaning products shut tight.
- Put small wastebaskets up where she can't get to them.
- Keep shoes in closets.
- Don't leave anything really valuable, like a first-edition book, on a low shelf where she could chew it.
- Check the garage for antifreeze, oil, cleaners, poisons, fertilizer, or paint and store them securely out of the way.

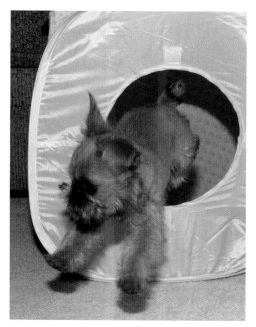

Puppies will explore your house.

It's important to make sure the collar is snug enough, because if something frightening happens while you are out walking, your dog will pull away, and if the collar comes off, she could run into the street. You want to make sure she is going to stay by your side so that if a big dog charges her, you can scoop her up in your arms.

Leashes: You need two kinds of leashes, a short, 6-foot (1.8-m) leash, and a retractable leash. The short leash should not be too heavy, and its clip should not be too big and heavy. Do not use a chain leash, as it will pull on the dog's neck. Other than that, Brussels Griffons do not care what kind of leash you buy, nylon, cotton, rope, or leather.

The retractable leash should be the small size, no more than 15 feet (4.6 m) long. It is easier to teach a Brussels Griffon to do her business outdoors if you walk her on this kind of leash. Brussels Griffon who have been raised properly don't want to relieve themselves anywhere near you. They want to get a distance away from you, sometimes even behind a bush or tree. The retractable lead gives her room to do this. She'll relieve herself, and come happily back without tripping or tangling the leash. Even Brussels Griffons who have their own backyard in which to eliminate need to be taught that they can go when on a leash. The retractable leash is a great training tool for this. One trade name is Flexilead, but there are many brands.

Identification tag: The best identification for your dog is a tag with your phone number inscribed on it. Several animal control officers have written up studies of their districts, showing that lost dogs who have a tag with a phone number on the collar are the most likely to be returned. If the numbers are big and easily read, the finder's first impulse is to call. Dogs without

Food and water dishes need to be wide to accommodate her broad head.

identification tags are more likely to be kept, or to be played with and then let loose again, or to be turned into a pound or shelter from which she may not return.

What You Will Need:

✔ Collar
✔ Leashes
✔ Identification tag
✔ Water and food dishes
✔ Bed
✔ Kennel crate
✔ Dog carrier
✔ Brushes and comb
✔ Nail clippers and styptic powder
✔ Scissors
✔ Chewable items
✔ Toys
✔ Bones

Therefore, buy a tag on which your phone number will be clearly displayed. It's best to put any other information on the other side of the tag so the phone number is as big as possible. On the other side, you might want to engrave the dog's name, your name, and your address, or a second phone number. Your cellphone number might be the best idea, as dogs tend to get lost when they are away from home. If she is lost, you are most likely going to be outside looking for her and have your cellphone with you.

Water and food dishes: Brussels Griffons need flat dishes at least 6 inches (15 cm) wide, because their big heads and pushed-in muzzles mean that they cannot eat from a tall, narrow dish. They would bump their foreheads. It's a good idea to put down a mat under the dog's water bowl, because her beard gets wet as she drinks, and water drizzles. Some Brussels Grif-

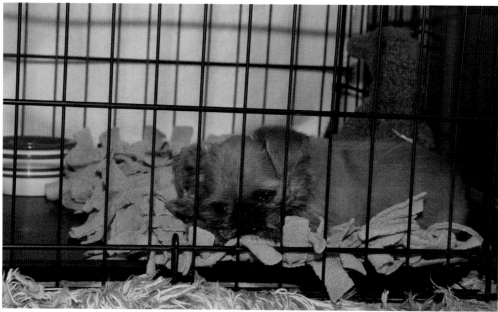

A puppy's crate is her den.

fons splash in water bowls in hot weather to cool off. If yours does this, buy her a baby swimming pool and put it outdoors in the shade. That will make her happy. Brussels Griffons quickly realize that splashing in water is amusing to humans.

Bed: A Brussels Griffon needs a comfortable bed to sleep in. Puppies need this bed in the room where they will stay when you are away from home. If you don't want her to sleep on your bed, your Brussels Griffon needs a crate or a bed in your room. If you are using a crate, get a thick, soft blanket or cushion to put in it. If you don't want the dog on the furniture, get a bed for the living room so that she has a place to relax while you are watching television. Most people who spend a lot of time on the computer keep a dog bed under the desk.

Brussels Griffons like donut beds (also called cuddle beds or cup beds), because they can curl up against the cushioned sides. But any kind of soft bed will do. For puppies, do not buy beds made of foam, as they tend to chew them apart and eat the foam. If they do, the foam usually comes out in the stool, but it could potentially cause a blockage. Lambskin fleece and faux lambskin beds are great.

Of course, the bed your Griffon will like most will be *your* bed. It's your decision whether or not she gets to sleep there.

Kennel crate: A Brussels Griffon likes a medium-size crate, not a really tiny one. But there are many great kinds. The size should be approximately 22 inches (56 cm) high, about 15 inches (38 cm) wide, and about 24 inches (61 cm) long.

Owners constantly debate whether crates with hard sides, made of plastic or wood, are best, or if wire cages are better. Crates with hard sides keep out drafts and bear more resemblance to the denlike setting of wild dogs. If you are ever going to transport your dog on an airplane, this is the kind you will need. In the Vari Kennel line, the #200 is the one required for Brussels Griffons, unless the dog is tiny, in which case you can use a #100. Wire cages let air pass through freely so the dog doesn't become too hot. Also, the dog can see you and you can see her more easily. If you decide on a wire cage, you can use a blanket to cover the sides to keep it warm in winter months.

Whichever one you decide on, place it in the kitchen or your bedroom or the room where the family gathers. Griffons like to be where the people are. The garage or the back porch are *not* good places for your pet's crate if you expect her to stay in it. The Brussels Griffon is strictly an indoor pet. And she needs a comfortable blanket, cushion, or crate pad to lie on.

Dog carrier: The dog carrier is a soft-sided nylon bag that you can use to take your Brussels Griffon with you wherever you go. It has strap handles so you can carry it over your shoulder, with the dog in the bag tucked under your arm. With a carrier, you can take your Griffon even places where she could not normally go, like on the bus or up in the elevator, because she is hidden. You are not carrying a dog, you're carrying a bag. Airline-approved dog carriers such as the Sherpa Bag can be used to transport your dog in the cabin of a plane. The bag is placed under the seat in front of you.

Various suppliers call these dog bags, dog carriers, or dog totes. For most Brussels Griffons, you'll want the medium size. They can be quite fancy, and some have wheels. Some look so much like a woman's purse that onlookers won't guess there's a dog inside. When buying yours, just make sure there is an adequate amount of venting so the dog can get plenty of fresh air.

Brushes and combs: New owners always worry about getting the right kind of dog brush. But in fact, there is no wrong kind. All brushes work well for grooming your dog. What's important is to groom her consistently, so acquire tools that you like to work with to make it a pleasant experience for both of you. A pin brush and a comb are necessary, but there are other kinds of tools to choose from

• A *pin brush* goes deep into the undercoat and gets out dead hair and dirt. It's made with round-end steel pins in a wooden or plastic handle.

Brussels Griffons never pout for very long.

• A *slicker brush,* with either wire or nylon spikes, is excellent for removing dead or loose hair from the dog's coat and undercoat. At the same time, it gives her skin a massage.

• An *undercoat rake* is a good tool to use on a Brussels Griffon, as it pulls out the thick, lighter-colored, soft-textured undercoat and leaves the dark red, wiry topcoat undisturbed.

• A *comb* is used for the dog's beard and the hair on her legs, which is longer than the hair on her body.

• A *curry brush* with rubber "teeth" is a good general grooming tool that can be used to rub in shampoo during your dog's bath. Curry brushes with ridged surfaces, like the ones used for horses, are for removing dirt and dead hair on very short-coated dogs.

• A *grooming glove* is useful for breaking up dried dirt on the dog's coat and massaging her skin. But this is an optional item; a brush is better at removing dead hair. A grooming glove can also be used to lift dog hair from the furniture and carpet.

Nail clippers and styptic powder: You'll use these tools for your dog's monthly pedicure. The most common type of dog nail clippers is the guillotine style, in which a stainless steel blade slides across an oval opening. The blade is replaceable when it becomes blunt. A blunt blade will pinch the dog's nail; a sharp blade slides quickly through the nail and doesn't pinch. The other type is the scissors style, which pinches and squeezes a little less because it cuts evenly from both sides of the nail. Some people use a nail file. You can purchase one contoured to the shape of dog toes.

Standard styptic powder is used as an aid to stop bleeding caused by clipping nails and minor cuts.

Should a Brussels Griffon Wear a Harness?

No, a Brussels Griffon should not wear a harness. Harnesses were invented for horses, dogs, mules, and cattle to pull wagons as a service to people. When you put a harness on a dog, she is able to throw all her strength into pulling. But the only thing a Brussels Griffon has to pull is you, which is not a healthy situation. Also, a harness is uncomfortable, as it circles the dog's chest and lungs. It rubs her and can cause a rash.

The correct apparel for a Brussels Griffon is a collar. Right from the start, train your Griffon to walk by your side on a loose lead. Your training will prevent her from pulling.

Scissors: The best scissors to use on your Brussels Griffon are those with a rounded tip that will not poke your dog. Use these for trimming hair around the eyes and around the bottom.

Chewable items: Small pieces of rawhide are the best way to keep your dog's teeth clean. A study was done over the course of ten years with three groups of Beagles. The first group got nothing to chew. The second group was given crunchy biscuits, like Milk-Bones, every day. The third group was given rawhide chews once a week. The results were conclusive: the group with rawhide to chew had far healthier teeth than the other two groups. As your dog chews rawhide or a similar substance, she massages her gums and cleans particles of food off her teeth. Older Griffons tend to lose their teeth, as do all toy dogs, so it's best to do what you can to help her your pet keep hers.

Toys: Griffs need small, soft toys or toys with parts they can grasp with their tiny mouths;

tennis balls are too big. Some cat toys make good Brussels Griffon toys, like stuffed mice.

Bones: Bones from the supermarket are a great treat, and a great way to keep your dog happily occupied. Ask the butcher to cut the bones to no wider than 2 inches (5 cm). Bake them at 350°F (177°C) for 20 minutes.

Additional Optional Items

Dog toothbrush and toothpaste: It can be difficult to brush a Griff's teeth, because any sort of pressure on her muzzle cuts off her air supply. For this reason, Griffons are reluctant to let you do this. A less invasive approach is to rub your dog's teeth with gauze.

Seatbelt: A seatbelt is just as good an idea for a dog as it is for you. This is the only situation in which a Griffon needs a harness, because dog seatbelts attach to a harness, not a collar.

Exercise pen: Like a playpen for a toddler, but usually metal, an exercise pen provides a place to keep your dog confined.

Puppy pads: These can be used instead of newspaper when housebreaking your dog.

Dog litterbox: This is the same thing as a cat litterbox, and is a relatively new idea in housebreaking. It's good for dogs who live in apartments.

Feeding Your Puppy

There is no subject as confusing to the new puppy owner as what to feed. There are so many brands of dog food to choose from, and different types: dry, soft, and canned. There is no one dog food that is perfect for every dog. How do you know what your puppy should eat?

The first answer is to ask the breeder, and buy the brand he or she recommends. The

Quality food is one of the ingredients of a healthy, happy dog.

breeder should give you a small amount of food to take with you when you pick up your puppy so that for the first three days she can eat what she is accustomed to eating.

The difference between an inexpensive dog food and an expensive one is the quality of the ingredients. The more meat and meat by-products in a food, the more expensive it tends to be. But there is an upside to this expense: the ingredients in the expensive foods are more readily digested and absorbed, so you need less. An inexpensive dog food is full of fillers that pass right through your pet. Therefore, dogs on inexpensive foods produce more and bigger stools. This is something to consider in an era in which

When Do I Feed?

Age	Frequency
2 to 6 months	Three times a day, morning, noon, and night, plus a 9 P.M. snack.
6 months to 1 year	Twice a day, morning and evening, with a 9 P.M. snack.
Over 1 year	Either once or twice a day, depending on your schedule and your preference.

we must carry plastic bags and clean up after our dogs in public places. The best stool is a small, dark, firm one. If your puppy is producing light-colored, soft, or runny stools and it is not due to worms or illness, then she is eating the wrong food. Buy a small amount of another kind and try it. Keep trying until you find a food that she likes and you don't mind cleaning up after.

A Healthy Diet

The best possible meal for a Brussels Griffon is a mix of dry food with meat and chicken or canned dog food. Be sure to get the "small breed" or "toy breed" size of whatever dry food

you choose. The kibbles will be small and easy for your dog to chew. Regular-size kibble is too big for her small mouth and teeth. A high-quality complete dry dog food is the best, because it is full of vitamins and nutrients. Foods that are labeled "complete" contain all the calories and minerals a dog needs. All the big-name dog food companies have carried out endless studies of what foods are best.

How much should you feed your dog? The amount varies, so try a quarter cup of kibble and a tablespoon of meat, chicken, or canned food. If she finishes it and seems hungry, increase the amount. Keep adjusting until she maintains a good weight in which her body is firm to the touch and her ribs well covered.

There are now "light" foods for dogs that need to lose weight, but fats are taken out to make them low in calories, and fats are necessary for shining coats. If your dog puts on weight, cut down the amounts she's eating rather than switching to a low-calorie food.

How often? A puppy should be fed three times a day. In addition, a snack at 9 P.M. is a good idea, because night is a long time for a little tummy to go without food. The 9 P.M. snack can be a few pieces of cut-up hot dog or meat, or two or three small biscuits or Milk-Bones.

Brussels Griffons charm us with their silly behavior.

Raw Food

Many people like to experiment with their dog's food. Some feed a raw diet. Most veterinarians and researchers do not recommend a raw diet because of the chance of bacteria. And, raw meat can be difficult to digest. Some owners feed their dogs only meat, on the grounds that in the wild, dogs ate only meat. But that has proven not to be true. Dogs in the wild first eat the stomach of their prey, which contains grains and vegetables. Also, dogs in the wild live short, brutal lives and never have shiny, healthy coats. You don't want your Brussels Griffon to look like that.

Food Allergies

Brussels Griffons tend to have healthy digestive systems that allow them to eat a range of foods without problems. The incidence of food allergies in Brussels Griffons is low. Common signs of food allergies are red, itchy skin, ears, or feet, persistent ear infections, diarrhea and vomiting, and raised bumps on the skin. The ingredients dogs tend to be allergic to most are corn, corn gluten meal, brewer's rice, wheat, any other grain products, and any sort of flavoring or preservatives, even if the food container claims the contents are "natural." There is no regulation of the word "natural" in pet foods. If you suspect a food allergy, be careful to buy foods that do not contain those ingredients. Instead, choose a food with a low number of grains and only one or two different meat protein sources (such as one with chicken and lamb, rather than chicken, turkey, lamb, and fish).

The First Day Home

It is common for a puppy to have a loose stool during her first day in a new home, due to the

Puppies are generally cooperative.

excitement and stress. This may also occur due to a change in food and water. If your puppy has a loose stool, give a teaspoon of Kaopectate. Also, put some plain yogurt on top of her food. Any continuous diarrhea could be a problem.

Special note: Because small dogs weigh so little, you must be very alert to any diarrhea or stomach upset, which can also cause dehydration. Be very attentive to your little puppy; if one or two doses of Kaopectate don't make her

She'll need time to get used to her new home.

better, see a veterinarian. Take the puppy's temperature rectally; the average should be 101.5°F (38.6°C). Anything over that, take her to the veterinarian. If she vomits more than once and is sluggish and subdued, bring her to the veterinarian. Although Brussels Griffons are tough little dogs, they are so small that illness can quickly affect them. (See more on this topic in the chapter "Health Considerations.")

Acclimating Your Puppy

Set up a schedule. Establish a routine for your new pet's feeding and exercise and follow it as consistently as possible. Like the rest of us, Brussels Griffons feel more comfortable if they

know what to expect. They like to know when during the day they will be taken out to eliminate. They like to know they can count on you to walk and exercise them. They get very excited when mealtime approaches. They are usually happier and more settled if these things happen every day at the same time. It's especially important to keep to a schedule when training a new puppy. When the alarm goes off at seven in the morning, get up and take her out. If you sometimes make her wait an hour or two, she may be forced to relieve herself the wrong spot, making your job of housebreaking much harder.

Be consistent. This pertains not just to the schedule, but also to everything you do with your dog. Decide on the rules the dog will live by and then stick to those rules. Dogs learn much more quickly and behave much better if you are consistent in your actions and expectations. Everyone in the household needs to agree on the rules for the dog. Can she sit on the couch? Is she allowed in the dining room? Should family members let her on their beds? Where should she relieve herself? Who will take her out for walks?

Be the pack leader. A leader is clear, concise, and consistent. Dogs understand and need to have a pack leader. If you don't assert your right to that position, the dog's instincts tell her she doesn't have to obey you. That means that the sofa is hers, the garbage is hers, the dinner on the table is hers, and the new shoes you just bought are hers. In short, she is in control. Leaders don't come when called. Leaders may bark when and how long they want. Leaders may bite. You don't want your dog to think

Teach your puppy to come to you so she won't get lost.

she is the leader, but she will if you don't show her that *you* are.

Praise. Praise is the reward the dog receives for obeying your command. Make the reward immediate. Reward the dog only for obedience. Don't praise her unless she earns it.

Boarding

You can't take your Brussels Griffon with you on every trip. First, ask a family member or friend to keep your dog for you. If that's not possible, there are many pet sitters who will come to the house twice a day. You can find ads for pet sitters at pet stores and veterinarians' offices.

If you need to leave your dog at a boarding kennel, try to get recommendations from friends who have had a good experience. Ask to see where your dog will be kept. It should be clean and comfortable. Ask if you can bring your dog's bed so she'll have that reminder of home.

Be positive. Tell the dog what you want her to do, not what you *don't* want. It is easier for the dog to understand one positive command, such as *"Sit,"* than a series of negative commands, such as *"Don't jump up," "Don't jump onto the sofa," "Don't bark."* Being positive reinforces the idea that you are the leader.

Don't get angry. You can't teach anything when you are angry. Yelling and shouting will frighten your Brussels Griffon, and it may take her a long time to trust you again. Anger never leads to the desired response. Deal with disobedience by using quick, matter-of-fact corrections. Don't get your emotions involved.

Enroll in training classes. Training classes help you communicate with your dog and build confidence in both the dog and owner. People who put in the effort to obedience train their dogs have fewer problems with them. A bond develops because of the time spent together. Just because you own a small dog doesn't mean that obedience training is not necessary.

Let her be a dog. Enjoy her, train her, have fun with her. Do not expect her to make decisions. That's your job—you're the leader.

Catching the Runaway Brussels Griffon

Even though they are small and have short legs, Brussels Griffons can be hard to catch if they don't want to be caught. They are quick and nimble and sometimes enjoy dancing just out of reach.

When you need to catch a dog, you must never run after her. Make sure she sees you, but then walk away in the opposite direction. When she follows you, stop, stoop down, and play with the grass as if examining something interesting. Do not look at the dog. If she comes close but not close enough, walk off in the opposite direction again. Curiosity will get the best of her and she will eventually come over. Don't grab the

Lost dogs are sometimes not returned, because the finder keeps them.

dog; talk to her and offer her the grass or a stick or anything to sniff and play with. You sometimes have to keep repeating this to bring the dog in. If you are desperate, lie down on the ground. No dog can pass by a person lying on the ground. When she comes over to sniff you, don't grab at her, because she will dance away. Instead, talk to her and offer her something to sniff or put in her mouth—things dogs like to do. If you think you can easily touch her, do it just with your finger, then pull it away. She will look surprised, as in, "Oh, is that all you wanted? I thought you were going to hurt me." When she is calm, touch her again. Build up little touches into a pat. Never reach for a dog until you have built up the little pats into strokes. At that point most dogs will give you their confidence and just lie quietly while you pick them up, as if saying, "Go ahead, pick me up, I don't mind. I thought you were going to grab me and hurt me!"

During the whole exercise, as soon as the dog is close enough to hear your voice, talk to her in a soothing tone. If you have a treat, put it on the ground, or leave it and walk way. Keep repeating this, shortening the distance until the dog is comfortable coming very close to get the treat.

The only time to "chase" a runaway dog is to get her away from a street. Then, flap your hands and yell at her to get her out of danger. When she is away from cars, then begin the "catch" procedure.

Identifying Your Dog

Many Griffons who are lost are never found because they were not wearing identification. Often, a lost Griffon is not returned because they are such sweet dogs that whoever finds

Griffs would prefer to be with you all the time.

Names for Brussels Griffons

Some names seem to go naturally with Brussels Griffons, here are a few

- Sprout
- Griff
- ET
- Wookie
- Chewy
- Gremlin
- Scooby
- Rascal
- Teddy Bear
- Ginger
- Ruby
- Lucy
- Pumpkin
- Teak
- Penny
- Pippin
- Pocket
- Rusty
- Reddy
- Tucker

one decides to keep her. This is especially true if the dog is not wearing a collar with a tag.

Microchip: A more permanent means of identification is the microchip, a rice-size pellet that is injected under the dog's skin between the shoulder blades. When a scanner is passed over the dog, it shows a number that leads back to you. As microchip technology becomes more widespread, there are stories of dogs being returned to their owners years after they were lost because someone checked for a microchip. The AKC recommends micro-chipping all dogs.

Tattoo: The other method of permanent identification is a tattoo, which is printed on

Sometimes, the right puppy will pick you.

the inside of the dog's thigh. It doesn't hurt, but the noise of the machine, the tickling feeling, and the fact that she doesn't like to be held still makes it a bit of a hassle to get a tattoo on a Griffon. A microchip, usually inserted by a veterinarian, is a better idea.

Either the microchip or the tattoo number is registered with an agency that can give the finder your address and phone number. There are several national registries with which to list your dog's number. The AKC runs a registry called Companion Animal Recovery, which is open 24 hours a day, 7 days a week, to help dogs find their way back to their owners.

The Lost Dog

If your Brussels Griffon is lost, go into action immediately. Report the situation to the police, as the finder might call them. Visit your neighbors. Call all the local veterinarians.

Get on the computer and make up a poster with your dog's picture on it, and pin up copies everywhere. It's best to put your cellphone number on it, in case a call comes in while you are out searching.

Many people don't know what a Brussels Griffon looks like, so when you call the pound to ask if your dog is there, you may be told "No," even if the dog is there. It's best to visit animal shelters yourself and look at all the dogs. Place ads in the local papers. Contact Brussels Griffon Rescue and ask to have a photo of your Griff posted on the organization's Web site.

A Brussels Griffon's Senses

When living with a Brussels Griffon, it's good to understand their sensory abilities, which differ from ours. They are clever, and have an uncanny ability to read our minds. They seem to have a "sixth sense" that allows them to anticipate our next move. But it could be the result of input from their highly developed five senses.

Sight: Their eyesight is calibrated to detect movement at greater distances than we can. But they can't see as well close-up. They can

Griffons have highly developed senses.

see well in very little light. But they can't see as many colors as we can.

Sound: Dogs hear about four times better than humans. They can hear high-pitched sounds, which is why they sometimes howl when we hear nothing at all. Brussels Griffons hear very well. They become alert when they hear a strange car in the driveway, turning their heads and pricking up their ears. They recognize a wide range of familiar sounds. When they hear the car or the voice of a friend, they often wag their tails. When they don't know the person, they are interested to find out who it is. They might bark when a stranger comes to the door, but in general, they don't make a lot of noise.

In addition to barking, some Griffons have other vocalizations, using a guttural sound to "talk," sometimes when they want something, sometimes when they stretch out on the sofa after a good meal, and sometimes to express contentment at being petted, to say they appreciate the attention.

Smell: A dog's sense of smell is highly developed. She smells many things we don't even notice. That's why Griffons snuffle in the grass

Why Do Brussels Griffons Rub Their Faces Into Pillows?

You will often see this behavior in brachycephalic breeds; it is caused by an itch in the crease between the dog's eye and nose, and is very difficult to reach. If your Griff does this, she needs your help. You must use your finger or a cotton swab to get in there and wipe out what is bothering her. It may be gummed-up dirt or moisture. Whatever it is, it needs to be cleaned. See the chapter on "Good Grooming" to learn how to do this.

Griffons are a toy breed, but not overly fragile and delicate.

and push their noses right up against people's ankles. They are getting a lot of information about what dogs have passed by or where the person has been. The dog's olfactory lobe is many times larger than a human's. According to one estimate, a human nose has about fifty scent glands. A canine nose has fifty thousand.

Additionally, on the roof of a dog's mouth there is a vomeronasal gland, something humans don't have at all. This gland connects to the olfactory function of the dog's brain and gives the dog the ability to "taste" scent. Sometimes a dog will become so excited about a scent, such as the scent of a female in heat, that saliva and foam slide around his mouth. This is because of the strong connection of the scent and taste functions.

When a dog detects an unknown scent, she usually lifts her head and begins to work the odor through her mouth. A UCLA researcher found that a police dog's sense of smell is six million times more sensitive than a human's.

Taste: Dogs have fewer taste buds than humans, which may be why they eat things that don't look appetizing to us, such as old meat and dead bugs. Some people say it's why its okay to feed dogs the same meal night after night, because they are not looking for a variety of tastes the way we do.

Sometimes a dog "grazes" in the grass, pulling out selected strands to chew. Her body is asking for some plant material, and the dog is filling that need. This often leads to vomiting. There may be something uncomfortable in the

Griffon admirers love their "monkey faces."

stomach and the dog needs to vomit to get it out. If she throws up grass and bile, don't rush her to the veterinarian; wait and observe her. She may have just solved her own little biological problem, not created one.

Touch: Griffons have a more highly developed sense of touch than other dogs. They love to be petted, stroked, tickled, and caressed. When they lie down next to you, they often like to touch you with a paw, as if to say, "I'm here!" They are also able to use their paws a little like monkeys, a very unusual canine trait. And many Griffons "hug," pressing themselves against their owners. Griffs share these traits with Affenpinschers, but not with other breeds.

Neutering and Spaying

Female Brussels Griffons go into heat starting from about six months of age, and every six months thereafter. During this period they may drip blood, although some females spend a lot of time cleaning themselves so that blood may not be apparent. The female's hormones demand that during this phase she seek a mate, so even those who normally stay happily at home may leave the yard in search of a male dog.

Male Brussels Griffons start to reach sexual maturity at around six months. At this age, they may start to "mark" their territory by urinating on selected spots. And the testosterone in their bloodstream demands that they travel to find a bitch in heat, if there is one anywhere in their vicinity. They also may hump other animals, objects, or people's legs.

These proclivities put dogs in danger, as they may cross busy streets or become lost as they follow the call of biology. It is far better to spay or neuter your dog. Consult with your veterinarian about the best age to do so.

Leaving Your Griffon At Home

No matter how much you love your Brussels Griffon and want to spend time with her, the time will come when you must leave her alone in the house. For a baby puppy, the very best solution is to provide a confined area, such as a corner of the kitchen, in a playpen or exercise pen. At one end, put her bed and water and food bowls. At the other, put down newspapers she can use to relieve herself. With toys and something to chew on, your puppy is set to spend the day alone while you go to work or pursue your normal life.

Their dark, wide-set black-rimmed eyes are large and expressive.

The most difficult thing about leaving a Griffon alone is how guilty many owners feel about it. But they shouldn't. Everyone works; if not, the bills won't get paid.

Also, dogs have a seemingly endless capacity to nap. Even wolves in the wild spend long hours of the day sleeping in their dens. Dogs don't have jobs, so they sleep. This is normal.

If you are regularly gone for more than about eight hours a day, you shouldn't have a dog. But a Brussels Griffon is perfectly capable of spending a normal eight-hour day without you.

As your puppy gets older, eventually she will be able to spend the time alone without going on the papers. When she can hold it all day, you may be able to give her the run of a room by herself, and eventually maybe the house.

Like other short-faced breeds, Griffons have trouble with temperature extremes. They cannot pant efficiently in hot weather, and their short nasal passages do not warm air efficiently in cold weather. A Griff must never be left in an outdoor kennel, even for a few hours, if there's a chance the weather might change.

Can Griffons Fly?

Griffons can fly! If you travel by plane, your Brussels Griffon can go along in a canine carry case. These are soft-sided carriers that look like gym bags except that they have netting on the sides to allow for easy airflow. Check the chapter on training to learn how to teach your Griff to love her carry bag.

What about the security checks at airports? The Griff and her carry case will be scrutinized,

just like every other bag. At the checkpoint the dog must be taken out of the carrier. The carrier goes on the conveyor for X-ray screening. The Griffon goes with you through the metal detector. Make sure there is no metal on her, because even her metal ID tag will ring the sensor. The only problem at security checkpoints is that all the officers want to pet the dog!

Once onboard, place the carrier under the seat. The dog can see you and hear you while she's out of sight. With her hyper sense of hearing and smell, she knows a lot more about what's going on in the plane than you do.

The airlines charge around $100 to carry your dog on the plane. That doesn't seem quite fair, because they don't charge other people extra for a gym bag of the same size. Many require health and rabies certificates. Check the airline's Web site or call to find out what the requirements are.

Some airlines don't allow dogs in the cabin, in which case they travel in the cargo hold. Many people panic at this prospect, yet thousands of dogs travel this way every year and arrive on time and in good condition. For this type of travel you need a hard plastic crate, one that is certified travel-safe by the airlines. A 10- to 12-pound (4.5 to 5.5 kg) Griff needs a #200 in the Vari-Kennel line of plastic crates. The rule is that the dog has to be able to stand up and turn around comfortably. You are required to fasten a dish in the crate and have the airline personnel fill it with water. The best idea is to put a few ice cubes in the dish, as they won't splash.

Airlines are required to keep the cargo area containing animals at the same temperature as the humans' cabin. After landing, the crates are brought to the baggage terminal and placed near the suitcases.

Dogs seem to stay awake during the entire plane trip, and then fall asleep quickly once they land. That's good, because a conscious dog can regulate her body temperature by panting. Never drug a dog before shipping. If she is too sleepy to pant, she could overheat.

Don't ship your dog on a hot day. If her crate has to be left out on the tarmac while waiting to be loaded, heat could be deadly. Most airlines won't let you ship a dog when the temperature is over 85°F (29.4°C). Because Brussels Griffons belong to the brachycephalic group of dogs, airlines are even more concerned about their ability to breathe in hot temperatures. Some airlines will take them only in cool weather; others refuse to take them at all.

GROOMING THE BRUSSELS GRIFFON

Brussels Griffons need regular grooming to be comfortable and look their best. Their monkey faces need washing and those long, cute beards must be combed and trimmed. An ungroomed rough coat becomes matted and unkempt. When the Griff is clean, he's happy, and his personality sparkles through.

Teaching Your Puppy to Enjoy Grooming

The rough-coated Brussels Griffon does not shed on your clothing or furniture, but the price for that convenience is that you must brush him in order to remove dirt and tangles. The first thing you must teach a puppy is to relax and enjoy his grooming time with you. Puppies know how to chew food, put things in their mouths, and jump on their mother. But no puppy was ever born understanding what it means to be groomed. Many people seem surprised when the puppy's reaction to his first few grooming sessions is to jump off the grooming table or crouch in place, trembling. This is simply his natural response to something that is unfamiliar to him. The solution is to show him that standing on the table while being groomed is *good* behavior. He doesn't know that, yet.

Grooming Table Behavior

First, you need a table with a surface that is not slippery; the best is a rubber, non-slip mat, but absent of that, a towel will do if you can make sure it isn't going to slide.

Place the puppy on the table but don't let him go. Keep your arms around him to make sure he doesn't jump off and hurt himself. What's important when you are teaching your puppy anything new is that you act as his confident leader. If he's scared when you put him on the table, simply hold him there for a minute and stroke him gently. Then give him a treat (a small piece of hot dog, for example). If he whimpers or wiggles, or does anything other than stand quietly, do *not* talk to him in a

Those long beards need combing.

stand on the table quietly for only a second, praise him, give him a treat, and put him on the floor. He will most likely be surprised and delighted, as if he's wondering, "Is that all you wanted?" You can give him another treat. Then pick him up and put him on the table again. Pet him there for a minute, give him a treat, and take him back off the table.

Brushing

After you've acclimated your dog to this procedure three times, he will feel that standing on the table is no problem at all. At that point you can pick up the brush and run it through his hair. If he doesn't like it, do it just once, give him a treat, and put him on the floor. You want to move only by baby steps and build a little on each one he takes. Soon enough he'll be a puppy who's happy to get up on the table and be groomed. He'll think that it's easy and fun, and he'll have confidence in you as his leader.

Let your dog sniff and examine the brush. Don't correct him if he wants to bite or chew it; that's his normal puppy response. You won't be leaving it anywhere he can get hold of it. Then, stroke him gently on his back with the brush, and give him a treat—just one stroke, followed by a treat. Staying still to receive a lot of strokes is a separate step. In your first few lessons, get him accustomed to letting you brush every part of his body. Talk to him in a normal voice. If he tries to get away or cries, do not comfort him. Comforting is a treat, and he will feel he was correct to cry or run.

How often should you brush your Griff?
Once a week is a good, though he'd be happy if brushed every day. Check to make sure there is

comforting voice, as people often do, saying things like, "Good boy, you'll be okay, don't worry." Your Griffon does not understand what you are saying; all he knows is that you are talking sweetly to him, and because what he is doing at that moment is crying or trying to get down, he thinks you are encouraging him in that behavior.

Your aim is to calm and relax your dog, so make sure that, as the leader, you are calm and relaxed yourself. Speak to your dog only in a voice that says "everything is fine." Do not comfort him; just show him that you are relaxed and that he should be, too. If he will

Weekly Grooming Routine

✔ Brush entire body with pin brush.
✔ Use a flea comb to check for fleas and ticks.
✔ Comb out leg furnishings and beard.
✔ Wipe around eyes with cotton swab.
✔ Trim hair around eyes.
✔ Trim hair around rectum or urinary areas.
✔ Swab ear canal.
✔ Clip tips of nails.

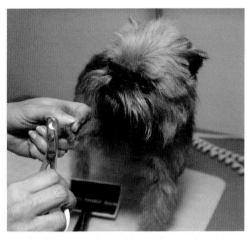

No Griff likes to have his nails cut, but it's necessary for good health.

no hair in his eyes and, at the other end, no hair stuck to the rectum or urinary areas; in both places hair must be kept short, or else it will mat and collect dirt, which will cause the dog discomfort. Use small scissors with rounded tips to cut away any mats or long hair in those areas.

Combing, Trimming, and Clipping

After your puppy has learned to accept the brush on his body, teach him to accept the comb on his legs and beard. Next, teach him to accept scissors (used for trimming hair around the eyes) around his head, by gently rubbing a closed pair over his head and then across his cheek.

The next lesson is to get your dog to relax while he is being clipped. Even if you plan on having him groomed by a professional, he will be much better off if he has learned not to mind the noise and feel of clippers, because groomers don't always take the time to teach this to a puppy; they have to get on to the next dog. If your dog won't relax he might have to be held down during the clipping process, leaving him

Grooming: Stripped for show (right); clipped for home (left).

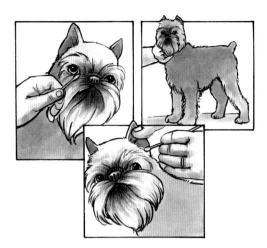

Clean the crease between the eyes and nose. Swab dirt from the ears.

the blade, along his side. Don't attempt to actually use the clippers until he is relaxed about this.

Ignore any bad reactions, and praise the calm ones and your Griff will quickly get the message. With these lessons, you will eventually have a relaxed dog who enjoys his grooming and does not fight to get away, making it much easier for you to keep him looking snappy.

When you are finished with grooming or a lesson, take some time to play with your dog. Your attention is the reward he loves the most.

Other Grooming Tips

With a cotton swab, clean the wrinkle between your Griff's nose and eyes, a place that is very susceptible to rash or infection. Check this area often.

Also, clip his nails every month with a nail clipper. Cutting dogs' nails does *not* hurt them; they are just sissies about it!

Ear Care

Cropped or uncropped, the ears need attention. Use a small amount of hydrogen peroxide or an ear-cleansing solution on a cotton tip to swab the inside of the ear. If there is a buildup of dark or red wax and a bad smell, consult a veterinarian.

Tooth Care

The healthiest thing for a dog's teeth is to brush them with a toothbrush and toothpaste, just as you do with your teeth. However, since their muzzles are so short, Griffs object more

terrified. So let him inspect clippers while they are turned off. Graduate to running the turned-off clippers over all parts of his body, praising him when he stands still and relax. Then, holding the clippers about 4 feet (1.22 m) away, turn them on. Speak normally to him to show him that the clippers are not scary. Turn them on and off. As soon as he relaxes and stands still, end the lesson. Take him off the grooming table. At the next lesson, move the clippers closer or turn them on and off while you are sitting on the couch with him to teach him to accept the noise. Graduate to running the clipper body, *not*

Grooming Tools
- ✔ Pin brush
- ✔ Comb
- ✔ Flea comb
- ✔ Cotton swabs
- ✔ Scissors
- ✔ Clippers
- ✔ Nail clippers
- ✔ Table with nonslip surface

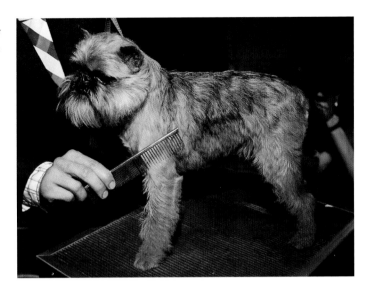

Show grooming requires long hours of dedication.

than most dogs to any fussing with their mouths. Putting any pressure on the side of his muzzle cuts off the air to his lungs, and he'll fight to get free because he can't breathe. An alternative is to rub gauze over the teeth to clean them. Griffs get a buildup of plaque on their teeth just as humans do, which leads to gum disease. The only way to thoroughly clean a Griff's teeth is when he is sedated on a veterinarian's surgery table. Like all toy dogs, Griffs tend to lose their teeth as they get older. Give him chews and toys designed to inhibit tartar and plaque.

Bath Time

There is nothing as sweet smelling and happy as a clean Brussels Griffon! However, Griffs are not big fans of baths, so make sure you hold him securely so he can't jump out.

Wet him down in a sink or bathtub, using a sprayer or cup to splash water all over his body. There is a wide range of shampoo products you can use. Choose a dog shampoo with an herbal scent you like, or use a baby shampoo or oatmeal shampoo. A dog's skin has a pH of 7.5 as opposed to a person's 5.5, but Griffs are not prone to skin rashes and allergies, so you can experiment. If your dog scratches and itches after a bath, that was the wrong shampoo, and you'll need to bathe him again with a different kind.

Work the shampoo into the coat, being careful to avoid the eyes. Use your fingers to shampoo his beard, which is the dirtiest part of the Griff. After rinsing, towel dry. In cold weather you can use your blow-dryer to get him dried off quickly.

You can bathe your Griff as often as you need to keep him clean and smelling good, but if you are brushing him regularly, he will stay clean and not need a bath more than twice a year. Griffons being shown have their beards and legs washed every day to keep the coat in those areas from breaking, but their bodies are not bathed to maintain the coat's proper wiry texture.

Bring a Picture

When you take your Griff to a professional groomer, bring along a photo of a well-groomed Brussels Griffon for her to copy. Griffs are rare and not every groomer has seen one.

Puppies are born dark, and change to red as they grow.

The coat is wiry and harsh.

Clipping and Trimming

In general, clip in the direction the hair grows using a #7 blade. Run the clippers over the dog's body from neck to thigh. In the front, hold the dog's head up slightly and run the clippers from his neck down to his chest, then over the top of the head.

Don't go over an area more than twice in an attempt to get it exactly even; doing so may cause clipper rash. You can do any fine-tuning with scissors or clippers with a #10 blade.

Tummy: To clip your dog's tummy, hold both of his front legs together and stand him on his back legs.

Ears: Change the clipper blade to a #10 and work in a downward fashion, both inside and out, then use scissors to trim the edges, as you can't easily get them neat with the clippers.

Legs: Comb the hair outward and then, following the leg's shape, use scissors to cut the hair in a downward direction about an inch (2.5 cm) from the leg.

Feet: Turn the dog's feet over and cut away any long hair, which can track dirt into your house.

Tail, rectal, and urinary areas: Use a #10 blade here. Go slowly and clip these areas only once so as not to cause a rash. If you are not confident enough with the clippers, use scissors.

Face: Hold your dog's head still by holding his beard firmly but gently. The face is the most important part to keep clear of hair; be sure there is none that can get in the dog's eyes and cause irritation. For the beard, comb out and use scissors to cut across it, leaving about an inch (2.5 cm). Some people like the look of a long beard, but a long beard needs to be cleaned fairly often.

Hand Stripping

Brussels Griffons shown in conformation must be hand stripped. This is a process of removing the dead coat with either fingers or a stripping knife, a grooming tool that is not usually available in pet stores. They are sold at dog shows and through some pet-supply catalogs. It is a time-consuming process because only a few hairs are removed with each pull.

The advantages to hand stripping are that the new coat that comes in is harsh and wiry, and dark red in color. Clipping sometimes leaves a soft or woolly coat, and sometimes a lighter color than rich, dark red. Both the National Brussels Griffon Club and the American Brussels Griffon Association have details about hand stripping on their Web sites.

A well-groomed Brussels Griffon.

Trim the beard with scissors.

Cutting the nails.

Cutting the Nails

There are four toes with nails on each foot, and sometimes another nail called a dewclaw a little way up the inside of the front leg. (The dewclaws are usually removed when the puppy is three days old.)

Keep nails short by using dog nail clippers. Be careful not to cut into the quick, the vein present in the center of the nail. If you do, it will bleed. But everyone nips the quick accidentally sometimes, especially on dark nails. If you keep the nail trimmed, it keeps the quick back.

If you do happen to make the toenail bleed, press it with a pinch of styptic powder and hold it for three seconds and the bleeding will stop. Griffons make a terrible fuss over getting their nails cut, trying to convince you that you are hurting them terribly. You will never get him to like having his nails cut, so just do it as quickly as you can and get it over with. If you take off the tips every week or so, the nail will stay short, and it is easier on the dog than having to cut a long nail.

A dog's nails should not click on the floor. They should not be sharp enough to scratch and gouge you. As a finishing touch, a little petroleum jelly adds a nice black gloss to the nails.

When you choose a Brussels Griffon, you are choosing a breed that is basically healthy. That is part of their appeal. They are not prone to many of the illnesses that plague other toy breeds. Griffons who are fed well, groomed regularly, have their faces cleaned and nails cut can live happily for twelve years or more.

Choosing a Veterinarian

It's important to have a good relationship with a veterinarian you trust. There is no shortage of vets in this country, so if you don't like one, try another. You want a veterinarian who will take the time to explain your dog's health to you.

Brussels Griffons are generally tough and uncomplaining about their doctor visits. After surgery, they recover quickly. They rarely growl or snap. They are sweet and forgiving, and a favorite with the hospital staff.

Not all veterinarians are on call 24 hours a day, so check with your veterinarian about what emergency clinic he recommends. Research the location of the clinic so you don't get lost on a night when you need to rush there.

Use as much care in choosing your dog's veterinarian as you would in choosing a doctor for yourself.

Health Matters

Even though Brussels Griffons are basically healthy, there are some canine illnesses that affect all dogs. To stay healthy, a dog needs vaccinations, parasite prevention, and an attentive owner. Your goal is to have your Griffon feeling at his best at all times.

Loose Stool

The problem most common to little puppies is a runny stool. With baby Brussels Griffons this must be watched very closely, because they are tiny and cannot afford to lose any body weight. A runny stool can quickly lead to dehydration, and dehydration can lead to death. Loose stool problems must be tended to immediately.

The usual cause of a loose stool in a puppy is a change of diet and/or the stress of moving to a new home. A puppy's stomach is producing the bacteria he needs to break down his food

Giving Medication

It is very difficult to get a whole pill into a Griffon, as his flat muzzle makes it hard to open the mouth and push the pill down. A much better idea is to crush the pill and put it into peanut butter, ground beef, liverwurst, cheese, or some other favorite food the dog will eat willingly.

It's important to remember that some medicines work best when there is a constant amount in the bloodstream, so do not miss any doses.

Administer liquid medicine with a syringe.

and digest it. When the food changes, it generally takes a few days for the stomach to catch up and start producing the right bacterial elements again. It's best to switch foods gradually, at first mixing a little of the new food with the old, and increasing the mixed amount for three days, at which point the tummy adjusts to the new food without a problem.

A puppy's stool should be firm and well formed. Anything else is a potential problem. As soon as you notice a stool that is loose, collect it in a plastic bag and take it to your veterinarian. He or she can determine the cause and administer the right medication.

Acute diarrhea in a puppy should not be treated at home. It really is important to seek veterinary help quickly, especially if the puppy is lethargic.

For an older dog with acute diarrhea there are some things that you can do at home that may be helpful. First of all, withhold food for a day and keep fluid intake to small amounts at a time. A good method of allowing access to small quantities of water is to put ice cubes in your dog's bowl.

It is usually okay to administer an antidiarrheal product such as Kaopectate or Imodium. For Kaopectate, the recommended dosage is about a teaspoonful per 5 pounds (3.2 kg) of body weight every two to six hours. You'll need a syringe. Squirt the liquid into the side of his mouth so he can swallow it. Don't force it directly down his throat, which could cause him to cough. A small amount of plain yogurt is also helpful if your dog will eat it.

If an older dog continues to have diarrhea after 24 to 36 hours, consult the vet. He will begin the process of finding and treating the cause.

Some possible causes of loose stool are described here:

Food: Very rich or fatty foods, such as liver or butter, can be the culprit, as can foods to which the dog is not accustomed, like milk or ice cream. Even foods that are basically fine, can cause a runny stool if the dog or puppy eats too much, as they will if offered quantities of, say, chicken or beef.

Digestive parasites: Coccidia are single-cell organisms that infect the intestine, causing a loose stool. These microscopic parasites are easily detected in a fecal test but are not visible to the naked eye. Coccidia cause a watery diarrhea that is sometimes bloody and can be life threatening to a Griffon, especially one who is small and young. The condition is easily treated by medication. Researchers have found coccidia in the stools of 30 to 50 percent of all puppies at some stage during their first few months of life. Most adult dogs have reasonably good immunity to coccidia.

Giardia is another protozoan parasite that is a common cause of loose stool in a dog. These small parasites come from the environment and live in any moist, shady area. They are very easy to miss in a fecal exam and sometimes are not even present in the stool of an infected dog. Repeated fecal exams are occasionally necessary to identify the organism. Signs of giardia infection include weight loss, inability to gain weight, diarrhea, vomiting, lack of appetite, and greasy-appearing stools. The medication generally used to treat the problem is metronidazole (Flagyl). Giardia is zoonotic, one of those rare illnesses that can travel from an animal to a human. Wash your hands after handling an infected puppy or dog. If a family member develops similar symptoms, see the doctor.

General cleanliness does not ensure that infections will not occur. Once coccidia and giardia are present in the environment, it is almost impossible to get rid of them. They can hide in even the cleanest and most carefully

tended kennel. Fortunately the medications to treat them are effective, gentle, and without harmful side effects.

Respiratory Concerns

Brussels Griffons are brachycephalic, that is, having a short-muzzle or flat face. Although, this trait helps account for their cute appearance, it brings with it certain special needs.

Brachycephalic breeds are more prone to heat stress than other breeds because they are not efficient at panting, the mechanism dogs use to

Dogs cool themselves by panting.

keep cool. A dog with a more conventional muzzle, like a Golden Retriever, is able to pass air over the tongue by panting, which begins the cooling process. Brachycephalic dogs are less able to get cool air into their systems. For this reason it's important to keep your Griffon cool, particularly in the summer months.

Griffs are also susceptible to a condition called stenotic nares, or pinched nostrils. Look directly at your Griffon's nostrils. They should be well open, allowing for easy breathing. If the nostrils appear closed and the dog pants or has trouble breathing, point this out to your vet. In some cases the dog needs an operation that involves snipping off the nares, the curved ends of his nostrils, or a resection, in which a small wedge of nostril is removed.

Most Griff owners will tell you that their dogs snore. Dogs who make excessive snorting or snoring noises may have a breathing problem caused by an elongated palate, a condition that is far more common in Bulldogs and Pugs than it is in Griffons; it can be corrected by laser surgery. Be aware of what degree of snorting and snoring is usual for your individual pet so you'll notice if anything changes.

Additionally, never let your Brussels Griffon become grossly overweight, as this could compromise his breathing even more.

Reverse sneeze: Occasionally a Brussels Griffon will snort and pull in air rapidly through the nose and seem to be gasping for breath. Owners always become concerned because they think the dog is having trouble breathing.

This is paroxysmal respiration, or what's called a reverse sneeze. It generally causes no harm and does not lead to any significant breathing problems, and usually goes away within a few minutes. It's caused by an irritation to the nasopharynx, a part of the throat just above the soft palate. It could be due to a speck of pollen or dust lodging in the throat; common causes are allergies, viral infections, excessive soft palate tissue, or nasal mites, but most often there is no identifiable cause. It's usually nothing to worry about. Sometimes you can help your dog by gently massaging his throat or blocking the nostrils briefly so that he breathes through his mouth, or by putting your finger on his tongue, which causes him to swallow.

If you think your dog is having a lot of reverse sneezing episodes, videotape him and take the tape to your vet. Dogs rarely display this behavior at the veterinarian's office, but a video will make it easier for the veterinarian to understand his condition and treat him.

Patella Problems

It is characteristic of small dogs to present problems with their patellas, or kneecaps, even in responsible breeding programs. All toy breeds are prone to this because of their small size; when the condition is really bad, the knees can be wobbly. Patellas can be too large, too small, or askew, or the groove that holds them in place can be too shallow, leading to a problem called subluxation, or partial dislocation. A subluxating patella is like a "trick knee": it can move out of place if jarred by jumping or tripping or injury. Veterinarians judge patella problems on a scale from one to five in order of severity; a five indicates a patella that is loose and may need surgery to pin in place.

Limping is a sign that something is wrong, so watch how your dog moves and make sure he does so in a manner that is easy, sound, and without pain. Many Brussels Griffons live their whole lives with subluxating patellas and are never lame.

If the kneecap pops out of place, it stretches the ligaments that hold it steady. If it happens often, the dog becomes lame. The first treatment is to keep the dog crated for several days and supervise his activity so he doesn't jump off furniture or steps. The veterinarian may give him prednisolone to bring down the inflammation that surrounds the knee. This period of rest may be all that is necessary to correct the situation.

Surgery is called for only when the condition is very serious and the dog is constantly lame, and should be done only by an orthopedic surgeon.

Eye Issues

If you decide to acquire a rough-coated Griffon you're going to have to take good care of his eyes, because he can't do so himself. Learn how to trim the hair from underneath his eyes; this practice will prevent the buildup of dirt.

Young Griffons should have clear eyes. Griff puppies sometimes have runny eyes and noses, much the way some children do, but they outgrow this tendency, as they get older. The best way to determine if a problem is developing is to take your dog's temperature.

It is not uncommon for older Griffs to develop cataracts, a clouding of the lens that causes light to scatter upon entering the eye. Another condition that causes cloudiness in the eyes of older dogs is nuclear sclerosis. Cataracts affect vision, while dogs with nuclear sclerosis can still see quite well.

Tooth Troubles

All dogs have 42 teeth. Brachycephalic dogs have less space to fit them in, meaning that the teeth are crowded and sometimes grow in at odd angles. Food debris is more easily trapped in their teeth, which leads to gum disease at a younger age. Like most toy dogs, Griffons lose their teeth, as they grow older, even with the best dental care. The good news is that they adapt to the lack of teeth very easily. They don't need special food. Their gums are hard, and they can still chew amazingly well.

Check your Griff when he is about six months old to see if he has a "double" set of canines, which means that the new ones managed to grow in without the baby teeth falling out. The veterinarian may need to remove the baby teeth.

Also check your old Griff for loose teeth, as they can cause infection in his gums. One ten-year-old stud dog, Pipp, was listless, losing weight, and seemed to be on his last legs. He had many loose teeth. The veterinarian put him under anesthesia to remove most of his teeth and gave him antibiotics. He quickly perked up and was his old self, and went on to sire many fine litters. The sore teeth and infected gums were the sole cause of his listless behavior and weight loss.

Ear Infections

A dog with an ear infection is uncomfortable. He will constantly scratch his ears and shake his head. But his methods won't work. It is up to you to treat the infection.

The most common source of ear trouble is ear mites. Symptoms are a reddish or dark brown discharge and an odor. Sometimes ear mites will create an environment within the ear canal that leads to a secondary infection with bacteria and yeast. The veterinarian needs to examine the dog and prescribe the correct drug. He may need to flush the ear.

There are several over-the-counter medications for ear mites, but they do not get rid of the egg cycle, so it's necessary to use them for thirty days in order to eradicate the mites. Veterinary prescription medications work at every stage, so treatment is a lot quicker.

It is important to get the medication deep into the ear canal. The dog's external ear canal is L-shaped. To medicate, gently pull the earflap to open the ear and put in a small amount of medication. Then use your fingers to massage the ear around the base. This helps the medication to get deeper into the ear.

Anal Gland Care

Anal glands are two small glands just inside the anus. Normally, the glands empty while the dog is defecating. But sometimes the sacs don't empty and become impacted and uncomfort-

Taking Your Dog's Temperature

A dog's temperature is taken rectally. Put a little petroleum jelly on a rectal thermometer. Hold the Griff on your lap and reassure him while you insert it. A normal temperature is 101.5°F (38.6°C), but one degree above or below that can be normal. If the temperature is over 102.5°F (39.2°C), take the Griffon to the veterinarian. A Griff with a high temperature will quickly become dehydrated, which is life threatening because they are so little. Medication will probably clear up the problem. Griffs are tough and recover quickly.

You are responsible for your Griff's health; he can't take care of himself.

able. Dogs with impacted anal glands usually scoot their rear on the ground in an attempt to empty them. They will constantly lick their anal area and chase their tails.

Most people prefer to have their veterinarian empty the glands, but it's possible to do at home. Hold a rag or tissue up to the anus and squeeze both sides. If the secretion is thick, this method may not work. Try putting on a rubber glove and lubricating your forefinger. Insert the finger into the anus and squeeze the gland between your thumb and forefinger. If this doesn't work, the veterinarian will have to do it. Impacted anal glands must be emptied or an abscess can form and rupture out through the skin.

Hypoglycemic Shock

Hypoglycemic shock is a sudden drop in the concentration of glucose in the blood. Glucose is the body's primary energy source. People who own Brussels Griffons need to know about this condition because it occurs without warning and, if untreated, can cause death. All toy dog breeds are predisposed to hypoglycemia, and more frequently in tiny dogs than large ones. It occurs more frequently in puppies than adults. Many puppies are lost every year to hypo-glycemia. It usually develops in young dogs from four to five months of age, but it can happen at any time. Some Griffon pups out-grow the hypoglycemia problem; as a puppy matures, his body is better able to store fat, his

Griffs are basically healthy dogs.

immune system is stronger, and his adult teeth are better for his consumption of food. Some need to be watched throughout their lives.

Symptoms: The puppy will be listless, weak, uncoordinated, and lethargic. He may be disoriented. Often the eyes are unfocused and barely open. He may try leaning against something because he is unsteady on his feet. He can't hold up his head. The gums and tongue turn grayish blue in color. The dog's temperature will be lower than normal. The puppy may shiver and tremble in the early stages. Then, he lies down and can't get up. Dogs often retain consciousness during hypoglycemic episodes but exhibit signs similar to a seizure. In an extreme case his body will become cold and he will lose consciousness. As the condition worsens, the puppy either goes into a coma or convulsions.

Death will result unless he is properly cared for immediately. The level of the blood sugar must be raised at once.

What to do if you think your dog is hypoglycemic: Hypoglycemia is an emergency and calls for an immediate administration of glucose. One commercial product you can use to address the problem ad hoc is Nutrical, but other glucose solutions are available. If you don't have one of those, Karo syrup will work, as will a few other alternatives: corn syrup, pancake syrup, honey, fruit juices, sugar solutions, infant formula, Ensure, or the like. Rub the glucose-rich supplement on the dog's gums with your finger or use a syringe to put it in his mouth. Put the puppy in a crate and make him rest. Beyond this, hurry to an animal hospital, because the puppy needs professional treatment.

In the hospital, the puppy will be warmed and his blood sugar level checked. The best method for delivering glucose is through an intravenous solution. Once the sugar hits the bloodstream, the puppy usually responds rapidly; he'll get up and wonder what all the fuss is about? The doctor usually keeps the puppy until he is drinking and eating well on his own.

Once your puppy has had a hypoglycemic episode, it is important to watch his food intake. Small meals every few hours will ensure that there's not a recurrence. If you think he hasn't eaten in a while and he's not interested in his dog food, offer him some chopped-up hot dog, sandwich meat, or cheese—anything to keep his digestive system going. If he's not drinking, dribble water into his mouth with an eyedropper or syringe.

Be aware of your dog's energy level. If your normally active puppy is suddenly sluggish, administer a glucose solution such as one of those mentioned above.

What to have on hand: Nutrical is a useful supplement; it is a gooey, flavored paste that contains sugar and vitamins. Some puppies will readily lick it off your fingers and others will take it only it if it is smeared on the roof of the mouth. If a puppy seems listless, the first thing to do is attempt feeding. If the puppy will not eat, put a little glucose supplement on the roof of his mouth.

Complicating factors: Sometimes there is more to hypoglycemia than just low blood sugar. Among these factors is, for one, bacterial infection. Bacteria can be tremendous consumers of glucose (blood sugar). For this reason, hypoglycemic puppies frequently are given antibiotics. Other factors include diarrhea, stress, and internal parasites. Stress from any cause increases the body's demand for sugar. This is why it is especially important to ensure the general health of the Brussels Griffon puppy. With the stress of a new home, new friends, or illness, it can be hard for him to maintain healthy blood sugar levels.

Sometimes an incident that looks like hypoglycemic shock is really a symptom of another problem. In young dogs it could be an indication of liver shunts, alanine deficiency, congenital hypothyroidism, or glycogen storage disease. When the hypoglycemia occurs in an adult, it could be an indication of insulinoma, pancreatic tumors, liver disease, or intestinal malabsorption. None of these diseases is prevalent among Brussels Griffons.

Other causes could be drug reactions or poison, such as antifreeze or rat killer.

Preventive Medicine

Preventive medicine includes vaccinations as well as treatments for heartworms and ticks and fleas.

Vaccinations

Your first trip to the veterinarian with your new puppy will probably involve vaccinations to prevent him from contracting any number of common diseases, such as distemper and parvovirus (discussed below). For the first eight weeks of life, the puppy is safe from disease thanks to the immunization he received from his mother by nursing. In the first two days, he ingests not milk but colostrum, a special secretion of the mammary glands that contains antibodies, vitamins, and minerals. It supplies essential immunity to the puppy and aids in the establishment of the intestinal function.

one vaccination, as human children do with just one vaccination against polio, diphtheria, measles, or smallpox.

Vaccines are made from the same germs that cause disease. When the weakened or killed germs are introduced into the dog's body, usually by injection, the immune system reacts to the vaccine the same way it would if it were being invaded by the disease: it makes antibodies. The antibodies destroy the vaccine germs just as they would the disease germs. They remain in the dog's body to protect him if he is ever exposed to the real disease.

Most veterinarians give "combination vaccines"—multiple vaccines given in a single shot. Some owners worry that it is not safe to give several shots at once, or that they may not work as well, or that they will overload the dog's system. But studies have shown that vaccinations are safe and effective when given together. The immune system is exposed to many foreign substances every day, and deals with all of them.

Shots are very safe, but they are not perfect. Like any other medicine they can occasionally cause reactions. Common side effects include soreness and redness at the injection site. Fever and muscle aches can occur. A severe reaction of anaphylaxis, or shock, is rare, but it does happen. Wait twenty minutes after a vaccination shot before leaving the vet's office, because if a puppy does have an anaphylactic reaction, he is quickly restored by an injection of epinephrine.

Just recently, Sooty and Sugar, 12 weeks old, got their second shots at Dr. Batts' office. The

But as that wears off, a vaccination is needed to boost the immune system's strength. Puppies generally receive three or four sets of vaccinations about once a month until they are four or five months old. At that point, the puppy's system is mature enough to create immunity that can get him through a year.

One year from his last puppy shot, the yearling goes back to the veterinarian for vaccinations to ensure his continued immunity to common diseases. After that first year, there is substantial debate in the veterinary community about whether or not a dog needs annual booster shots. Most vets recommend them. But recent long-term studies show that older dogs maintain antibodies for many years after just

Be alert to your Griff's energy level so you'll know when he's not feeling well.

breeder chatted with the staff and waited twenty minutes before leaving. The puppies were fine. Four hours later, Sooty collapsed on the floor. Dr. Batts advised giving him three milligrams of Benadryl, which meant crushing a 25-milligram tablet into powder, then putting a few drops of it into peanut butter and sticking it to the top of the dog's mouth. Shortly after receiving the medication, Sooty revived completely and became his energetic little self again, pouncing on his sister, splashing in the drinking water, and grabbing some kibble to chew. He had had a delayed anaphylactic reaction.

Heartworm

Heartworm is a potential problem in most areas of the United States. But preventing it is easy with a daily or monthly treatment of ivermectin. In northern states, veterinarians often recommend using heartworm pills for the summer months and testing the dog every spring before starting the medication again. In warm climates, dogs stay on heartworm medication year round. It's important to keep dogs protected against this possibly deadly parasite.

Fleas and Ticks

With the new treatments available, fleas can be banished from your dog and your home. Dogs are treated monthly with a drop of medication between the shoulder blades. This effectively kills off the fleas.

Ticks are a more difficult problem. If you live in a tick-prone area, you need to check your dog every day and remove any ticks from his skin. The most dangerous ones are deer ticks, tiny insects that can carry Lyme disease. Take a pencil and make a dot on white paper; that's

With preventive measures, he'll be free from fleas.

who contract distemper often reaches 80 percent. The disease also strikes older dogs, although less frequently.

Even if a dog does not die from distemper, his health may be permanently impaired. The disease can leave a dog's nervous system damaged, along with his sense of smell, hearing, or sight. Pneumonia frequently strikes dogs already weakened by a distemper virus.

Distemper is highly contagious. It is so prevalent and the signs so varied that any sick young dog should be taken to a veterinarian for a definite diagnosis. The good news is that the vaccination against distemper is extremely effective.

Parvovirus: Parvo is another highly contagious viral disease that attacks the intestinal tract. The first signs are depression, loss of appetite, vomiting, and severe diarrhea. These signs will most often appear five to seven days after the dog has been exposed to the virus.

Dogs dehydrate rapidly due to vomiting and diarrhea. Most deaths occur within 48 to 72 hours following the onset of symptoms. Death can occur as early as two days after the onset of illness. There are no specific drugs that kill the virus in infected dogs. Treatment of parvo, which should be started immediately, consists primarily of efforts to combat dehydration by replacing electrolyte and fluid losses, controlling vomiting and diarrhea, and preventing secondary infections with antibiotics.

In the past, a high percentage of pups less than five months old died from this disease. Now, due to widespread vaccination, these percentages have decreased dramatically.

Kennel Cough: Kennel cough is formally known as tracheobronchitis. The cough can be slight and occasional, or it can be severe and chronic. Sometimes dogs develop a nasal dis-

how big a deer tick is. You can't see it or feel it on your dog. Your veterinarian will know if there are Lyme disease-bearing ticks in your area. He may recommend vaccinating your dog against this illness. You also might consider having your trees treated to keep ticks away.

Common Canine Illnesses

It's easy to forget how serious some canine illnesses can be because we don't see them much anymore. Distemper and parvovirus used to kill thousands of puppies in the United States every year. With vaccines, this is no longer the case.

Here are descriptions of some of the most common diseases vaccinations guard against:

Distemper is the greatest single disease threat to dogs. Young dogs and puppies are the most susceptible. The death rate among puppies

charge. Transmission occurs by contact with the nasal secretions of infected dogs, so when one puppy in a litter gets it, they all usually do.

Vaccination can be done by the use of a nasal spray or an injection. While nasal sprays are a good choice for dogs with long muzzles, Brussels Griffons, with their short noses, are particularly frightened by nasal spray. An injection is often the better choice for a Griff.

The vaccine protects the dog against the strain of kennel cough caused by the bacterium *Bordetella bronchiseptica*. The problem is that there are dozens of other types of bacteria that cause kennel cough. The condition is usually minor in an adult dog, but takes a long time to clear up, two to three weeks or more. The veterinarian prescribes antibiotics to make sure it does not turn into pneumonia. Kennel cough in puppies is extremely dangerous and needs to be treated immediately. They don't have the strength to fight the infection.

Most boarding kennels require dogs to be vaccinated against bordetella.

Parainfluenza is caused by a virus that produces a mild respiratory tract infection. It is often associated with other respiratory tract viruses. In combination, these viruses are usually transmitted by contact with the nasal secretions of infected dogs. The vaccine to protect against this disease may be combined with other vaccines to offer broader protection.

Rabies is a terrible infectious disease that affects not only dogs but also wildlife and humans. Raccoons and bats in particular contract rabies, and in some areas the infected animals attack pet dogs in their own backyards. A virus that enters the nervous system causes

Full of self-importance.

the disease. It is transmitted by a bite from a rabid animal.

Vaccination against rabies is required in every state. Improved rabies vaccination and animal control programs have dramatically reduced the number of rabies cases in this country. Many cities and counties offer free rabies vaccinations at yearly clinics.

The majority of recent human cases in the United States have resulted from exposure to bats.

Lyme disease is transmitted by the tiny deer tick. The symptoms of Lyme disease vary widely, and it is often misdiagnosed. Often, the bite by an infected tick will swell, and there is often a

The high-set tail shows his alert, keen nature.

red rash in the shape of a target. However, sometimes there is no rash, or it is small and not noticed. As Lyme disease develops, the symptoms include painful joints and flu-like illness. There is a Lyme vaccine, but even vaccinated dogs have come down with the illness.

Heart Murmur

A murmur is an extra sound with each heartbeat. Your veterinarian can distinguish between benign murmurs and those that could signal an abnormal heart condition.

Small heart murmurs are not uncommon in puppies of the toy breeds. These are called "juvenile" heart murmurs, and they disappear as the puppy grows and his body and organs develop.

Heart murmurs among adult dogs vary widely in their significance. A heart murmur in a dog that seems normal in all other respects doesn't mean the dog should undergo a lot of expensive testing. But it does make it important for the owner to watch carefully for signs of heart failure, such as tiring easily, coughing, weight loss, and difficulty breathing. If any of these other signs are present, then it is crucial to try to identify the cause.

Murmurs are graded in severity from one to six, with one being the softest murmur that can be heard and six being loud enough that it's strongly evident. If your dog has a strong murmur and other signs of heart trouble, the veterinarian will take chest X-rays and possibly refer the dog to a canine cardiologist, who might run an electrocardiogram and an echocardiogram to find out if there is a problem.

Should you worry if your dog has a heart murmur? Not necessarily, because less than one percent of heart murmurs are a sign of problems. Griffons are not commonly affected by malformed hearts or valvular degeneration, as are some other toy breeds. Dogs with murmurs can live long, active, happy lives.

When to Call the Vet

✔ Loose stool for more than half a day
✔ Repeated vomiting
✔ If you suspect any kind of poison
✔ Severe breathing distress
✔ Bleeding from any part of the body
✔ Sudden collapse or loss of balance
✔ Extreme lethargy
✔ No interest in food, skips meals
✔ Eyes red or swollen
✔ Severe itching causing red spots
✔ Rectum red and swollen

Anesthesia

Many people worry about anesthesia, which is used during neutering or spaying or other surgery. But veterinary anesthesia today is generally safe, because veterinarians have available for use drugs that are short acting and reversible. In general anesthesia, an intravenous catheter is placed in the throat so that emergency drugs can be administered without delay should the dog have an adverse reaction. It also serves to keep the passageway open for air.

Brussels Griffons, like all the brachycephalic dogs, require extra care when coming out of anesthesia because in a heavily drugged state, their elongated soft palates or tongues can block air from getting to the lungs.

One veterinarian, Dr. Sharon Jackson, recalled that fresh out of veterinarian school she removed the tube too quickly from the first Pug she operated on, and his tongue slid back, blocking his airway. She held the Pug's tongue for 15 minutes until he became alert and was

breathing easily. She never forgot that lesson and thereafter always left the tube in for extra minutes on all the short-faced breeds.

Brussels Griffons are a breed that veterinary surgeons will monitor closely after a procedure. Because of their general good health and plucky nature, Griffons usually recover quickly from surgery and the effects of anesthesia.

His expressive face has humanlike qualities.

The very best thing you can do for your dog is to be aware of his behavior and patterns. If he doesn't eat his dinner; if he is sluggish and weak; if he is a usually happy dog who suddenly seems depressed—all of these are signs that only you can notice and interpret. The more information you can give the veterinarian, the better the veterinarian can diagnose the problem.

To examine your dog, place him on a table so you can do so easily. Frame his face with your hands so you can see it clearly.

Eyes and Nostrils

Look into your Griff's eyes. They should be clear and bright, with no tears streaming down his face. If there is sticky matter around his eyes, wash it away gently with warm water. If hair is matting around the eyes, trim it away.

Check the dog's nostrils. Young puppies often have runny noses, which is not a sign of illness, but there should be no pus or discharge other than a slight, clear liquid. If the nosepad is hard and crusty, put on a dab of petroleum jelly or butter on it to keep it soft.

The dog's breathing should be regular, with no rattling or wheezing noises. He should not gulp for air. The normal respiratory rate for dogs is 16 to 20 breaths per minute.

Teeth and Ears

Check your Griff's teeth from the side; never try to open his mouth from the front, because it cuts off his breathing and will cause him to panic. Gently lift the gum on the side and look for loose or infected teeth. For a puppy of around six months of age, check to see that no baby teeth have been retained.

Use a cotton swab to check the dog's ears. There should be no smell, wax, or discharge. If there is, clean gently. If he persistently scratches his ears he will need treatment for mites or other infection.

Rectums

Check your dog's anal end to make sure it is not red and swollen. Clear away any matted hair.

Body, Skin, and Feet

Run your hands over your Griff's body; it should be cool and firm to the touch. If the dog is unusually hot and there are other symptoms of illness, such as vomiting, diarrhea, or lethargy, you need to take his temperature. If his body is very soft to the touch he may be overweight, which is not healthy. Make an adjustment to his diet and get him out for a walk every day.

Your Griff should allow you to turn him on his back and stroke his belly while you check the condition of his

Health check: nose, eyes, ears, rectum, and feet.

DOG'S HEALTH

skin and genitalia. You should be able to touch all parts of the dog's body easily. If your touch causes pain, try to figure out what's wrong.

His skin should be pink and clear. Fortunately, unlike many toy breeds, Griffs are not particularly prone to sensitive skin conditions. Nonetheless, check for any red spots, which could be signs of cuts, sores, or infections. Cuts should be cleaned with an antibacterial ointment. If red spots persist, the veterinarian may need to take a scraping to test for ringworm or mange. Mange is caused by various species of mites, tiny eight-legged pests related to spiders.

If your dog's been good so far, give him a treat. He deserves it, and you want him to welcome your exams, not be afraid of them.

Griffs generally don't like having their feet handled, so you'll have to get your dog used to it. Feel the bottom of his pad with your finger to make sure no stones or thorns are caught between his toes. You'll usually be able to tell if something is wrong with his feet, because he'll limp. A possible cause is letting the nails grow too long; when this happens they curve back and rub or puncture the pads of the toes.

Pain

For pain, particularly pain caused by arthritis, half an aspirin usually works for dogs. Do not give acetaminophen (such as Tylenol) or ibuprofen (such as Advil), which can interfere with the normal function of the liver and cause problems.

Giving a Pill

To give your Brussels Griffon a pill, grind the pill into powder. Mix the powder into a dab of peanut butter and smear this on the roof of his mouth.

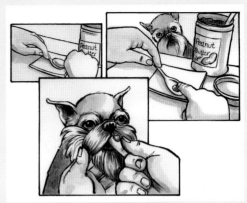

Crush the pill with the back of a spoon. Mix with peanut butter and smear on the roof of the dog's mouth.

The Brussels Griffon is not a common breed, so not every veterinarian is familiar with these dogs. It is wise to consult your Griffon's breeder or another owner with questions about his health. Another source is the Internet; there are Web sites devoted to Brussels Griffons and other toy dog breeds. People who live with Griffons for years know a lot about their health and care and may be able to put your mind at ease or alert you to a potential problem.

First Aid Kit

Basic items to have on hand should include:
- Veterinarian's emergency phone number
- Thermometer
- Antiseptic skin ointment
- Nutrical or other paste for hypoglycemia
- Kaopectate and syringe to administer it
- Benadryl for allergic reactions
- Ophthalmic ointment
- Petroleum jelly

SECRETS OF SUCCESSFUL TRAINING

Brussels Griffons take well to training because they are intelligent and love to please. A Brussels Griffon with good manners is a good reflection on you.

Stewardship

When you buy a new puppy, you have taken on the stewardship of a living being. She cannot provide anything for herself. She is totally dependent on you. On the day you pick her up from the breeder, she knows how to be with her mother and how to play with her siblings. She knows how to eat on her own. She knows how to walk. She may or may not know how to relate to other dogs. But she does not know much else.

From the very first moment you bring her home, your puppy is starting to learn. Sometimes we are not aware of that. But everything that happens to that puppy, even in her first day with you, is a learning experience.

Housebreaking

The first thing your Brussels Griffon needs to know is where she is to eliminate. The best way to teach her this is to be consistent right from the start. When you get her home for the first time, chances are she has to pee. Take her to the designated spot, whether it's outside or on newspapers, and wait till she relieves herself. When she does, immediately give her a treat.

When you have your dog indoors, keep her to a confined area. If you don't, she will wander off, investigating the far reaches of the house, and she will pee somewhere while you're not looking. If she does, she has just learned a lesson: that it's okay to pee in a corner when no one's looking. You must keep the dog near you so she can learn that it is *never* okay to pee in the house.

Take a young puppy out every two hours. It's best if you take her to the place where she peed last time. The minute she eliminates, praise her and give her a treat. This will cement in the puppy's mind the idea that going outside is good.

A young puppy will have accidents in the house. That's life. If you catch her in the process, say "No!" and pick her up and take her out. But never yell at or hit her. Griffies are very sensitive to correction, so it doesn't take much for the dog to get the idea. She'll learn quickly with the praise and reward system if you are consistent and work with her constantly.

Until your puppy is at least six months old, take her out frequently and generously praise and reward her for the right behavior.

Treats

It is important that the reward your dog gets for good behavior is something really delicious. That means meat. Dogs love meat. The easiest way to provide it is by cutting a hot dog into small pieces and keeping them in a plastic container. Bring the container from the refrigerator quickly whenever a training situation arises. The most important one is housebreaking. Take the container with you when you take the puppy outside to do her business, and give her a piece of hot dog as soon as she does. If you are paper training, grab the treat container when you see her starting to squat on the paper and give her a treat when she does. Giving a really delicious

Housebreaking Tips

- Allow your dog as many chances as possible to go outdoors—a minimum of once every two hours during her first weekend with you.
- Restrict her to a small area where you can watch her.
- Always go to the same area.
- Always give a treat and lavish praise for correct behavior
- Use cue words such as "potty time," "take a break," or "do your business."
- Look for telltale signs that the dog is about to go, and remember them.
- Set up a bell at the door. Show the bell to your dog and attempt to get her interested in it before each outing.
- After each success outdoors, allow your dog a short period of freedom, either outdoors or indoors, as a reward.

treat is the quickest way to show your dog that she's done the right thing.

You could also use cut-up chicken, beef, or cheese. The most delicious possible treat is liver. If you use it, feed only a small amount, as it's very rich.

Hard dog biscuits can be used as treats, but these aren't as good as your dog is not as highly motivated to get them, and they require time to chew before continuing the lesson.

Crate Training

A crate is an indoor doghouse, just big enough for the dog to stand up and lie down and turn around in. It's your dog's den, the

Use small treats as rewards.

Housetraining takes persistence.

place where she can feel safe. When you go shopping, or when your pup is very young, it's the place where she waits so that she keeps out of trouble. However, don't expect a very young puppy to stay in there for long periods of time. Keep the crate time to short intervals and extend them gradually as the pup gets older. When your puppy is very young, if you must be gone for an extended period, leave the crate door open and place newspapers nearby.

How long can my puppy stay in the crate? For a few hours while you go shopping, or overnight when it's placed next to your bed. If you are going to be gone for a long time, you should get a pet gate and confine the dog to a gated area where she cannot pull lamps off tables or chew electrical cords. You'll also have a place to keep her if you have guests who don't appreciate dogs.

Where is the best place to put the crate? The busiest room in the house, wherever the family congregates. Brussels Griffons are social animals. They need to feel that they are a part of the family.

Taking trips: Once your dog is crate trained, it will be easier to take her along on trips. She will get accustomed to traveling in her crate in a vehicle, and will handle the stress of being shipped if necessary.

Leash Training

Brussels Griffons can be stubborn about walking on a lead, so it's best to approach this training through baby steps. First let the dog run around wearing a collar for two or three days, until it comes to feel natural to her. Then, attach a light leash and let her drag it around the kitchen. When she doesn't mind that anymore, pick up the leash and *you* follow *her*. This gets her used to the feeling of having someone holding a leash. Get out your treats, and with a

Leash training.

What Your Brussels Griffon Can Teach You

✔ When loved ones come home, run to greet them.
✔ Always use your best manners. You will get more treats.
✔ Take lots of naps.
✔ Stretch before rising.
✔ Be thankful for a pat on the back.
✔ Play nicely with others.
✔ Don't let the big guys run you off. Just because they're bigger doesn't mean they're better.
✔ When you're happy, dance around and shake your entire body.
✔ When you are scolded, pout for a few minutes but get over it and get back to having a good time.
✔ Eat with enthusiasm.
✔ Be loyal.
✔ Never pretend to be something you're not.
✔ Be supportive of your friends, particularly when they are having a bad day.

very gentle tug, ask the dog to follow you. And give her a treat when she does. Griffs often fight walking on a leash at first, so early lead training is important. They do not quickly forget a traumatic experience; so keep training upbeat and pleasant. Be calm, use treats and toys, but don't pull or yank or your Griff will be terrified.

Walk with Me, Come to Me

The most important thing your Brussels Griffon needs to learn is to come to you when called. There is no trick to it; like all dog endeavors, it is the result of practice, day after day, of something very simple. When your puppy is young, take her out in the backyard or to the park, pick her up and carry her to the middle of the field, put her down, play with her, and walk away. At that young age, puppies have a built-

in instinct to follow. Let her follow you, then bend down and give her a treat. Keep walking and repeat the stops for treats. Now and then the puppy might fall behind or make a bit of a dash in the wrong direction, but she will *always* turn around and come with you. After a short distance, either sit down or bend down and give her a treat and play with her.

After a brief rest, stride off again. Your puppy will fall into line behind you. After about 20 feet (6 m), stop and repeat the treats and playing. Then start off in another direction.

Many people say, "I don't have time for that!" But you must make time. This lesson in freedom is very important in the dog's life. You want the dog to learn that it doesn't matter whether she is on a leash or running free; it is all the same. She will be in the habit of following and coming to you.

The best training is done with puppies when they are young. With an older puppy or dog, do the exercise with the dog on a retractable lead. This gives her a lot of freedom without worries that she will run off. Eventually you can graduate to off-leash walking.

It is much easier to take the time from the beginning to teach the dog that freedom is no big deal and that when you walk off, it's best to go with you. Your dog is only going to be as well behaved as you teach her to be. She needs your time and attention. Lessons from her childhood will pay off throughout her life. Spend the time. Start now.

Humping Behavior

Humping is usually a sign that your dog's hormones are telling him that it is time to reproduce. Puppies in a litter hump each other constantly. It may be that they are learning early pieces of mating behavior. But they are also doing it for dominance. The puppy who can hump another puppy is dominant over that puppy. Puppies fight each other constantly to "be on top."

Both male and female dogs hump in an attempt to assert dominance. When they don't have littermates or other dogs, they may hump stuffed toys. Humping can also be play, rather than sexual or dominance behavior.

Neutering or spaying removes the source of hormones, and usually lessens or dissipates humping behavior. Train your dog not to do this by saying *"No!"* and refusing to pay attention

Walk with me.

to him. Your Griff wants your attention, so being ignored is a punishment. He will learn that as soon as he humps, he gets no attention, which makes him unhappy.

Biting

It is normal for a puppy to grab and chew on people. If she were living with her littermates, she would be chewing on them and on her mother. It is natural dog play. But it is not okay to put her teeth on people, so you must have a response that lets her know that. To train her, you must get her to do the biting behavior so you can show her that it's wrong.

Draw the treat back over her head and help her to sit.

and cradle her in your arms on her back. The first time you do this, a Griffon will panic and fight because this is not a normal position for her. It feels very strange and uncomfortable at first. Hold her in this hug, telling her she's okay and everything is fine, just until she settles down and lies quietly in your arms. The instant she quiets down, say, "Good girl!" and put her down. Don't try to keep holding her for several minutes, because if she's already scared, she will only feel more scared. This exercise is done in small increments. When you put the dog down, she will connect getting what she wants (to be put down) with her relaxed behavior.

Repeat this every day. You can certainly do it more than once a day. If you are consistent, in a few days it won't scare your Griff to be held in this way. She'll relax, and that is your goal. This will make it easier for her to trust you and will ensure that she will be calm when you have to carry her, especially if you are in an emergency situation and don't want her to fight with you as you rush out of the house. It will also teach the dog to accept her doctor's handling of her body.

Good Training Tips

1. Exercise your dog before training to burn off excess energy that will keep him from concentrating. With a Griff, a short walk will usually do.

2. Train before meals, when he's hungry.

3. Make training fun.

4. Be sure he understands what you want.

5. Work in baby steps.

6. Never get angry or yell.

7. Celebrate each thing he learns with praise and play.

8. Always end a lesson on a positive note.

Sit down to play with your puppy, with a ball or tug toy or whatever she likes. Speak to her playfully in your normal voice. The minute a tooth touches your skin at all, say "Uh-oh" or "No" in a calm voice and walk away from your pup. The play session has just ended, which is a punishment for her. After this is repeated many times she will understand that the fun stops when teeth are used.

The Baby Hug

A good way to teach your Brussels Griffon to allow herself to be handled is the baby hug. Starting from the first day, pick up your puppy

Teaching to Sit

Put him on a leash, so he can't dart off. You'll need to get down to his level. Make sure his attention is focused on you. Show him that you have a treat in your hand. Hold your hand just in front of his nose. Give the command, *"Sit."* Move your hand backward over his head so as he looks up and tips his head backward, his hips sink to a sitting position. Use your other hand to guide him into the sit. As soon as he sits, give him the treat.

Say, "Okay," and let him get up and walk around while you praise him. Then repeat the exercise. A light bulb will click on when he realizes that sitting is the way to get the treat. When he understands and willingly offers the sit, ask for it at different times in the day and in different locations.

A good sit is a marvelous training tool, because you can use it to distract him when he's doing something you don't like. Instead of yelling, "Stop chewing on that book!" ask him to sit. Replace the bad behavior (chewing) with the good behavior (sitting).

Teaching to Lie Down

Put him into the sitting position, but instead of giving him the treat, put your hand in front of his nose and draw it downward between his front legs. As he sinks to follow your hand, let him have the treat when his elbows touch the ground. Don't worry if he pops up quickly the first time. Just praise and train again. When he realizes you want him to lie down, add the command, *"Down."*

Teaching to Stay

Ask the Griffon to sit, but do not give a treat. Instead, put your open hand in front of his face

Lure her with the treat to lie down.

and say, *"Stay."* He may be surprised and pop up. Ask for the sit again, and if he will stay seated just for a moment, tell him, *"Good dog!"* and give the treat. Each time, ask for a slightly longer stay. Extend the time in small increments.

Stay!

Two Kinds of Walks

There are two kinds of walks. The first is walking in order to relieve himself. For this, walk him on a loose lead or a Flexilead, letting him sniff trees and grass to find just the right spot. Allow him a few minutes to find the right spot and do his business.

The second kind is walking for exercise, or to get somewhere. For this, shorten the lead, tell him, *"Let's go,"* and encourage him to walk with you. Walking along at your side is the desired behavior, so when he does this, he gets a treat. For this walk, you decide on the pace and where you will go, not the dog. All dogs will try to convince you that they absolutely have to stop and sniff and might have to pee, but this is not the right time. You have already allowed him time to relieve himself. He does not have to do so every few minutes. His job now is to walk with you, with stopping only when you do. He will try to convince you to stop at every light pole and fire hydrant. Your job is to keep going, giving him a brief tug, and the command, *"Let's go."* He will soon learn to distinguish between the two kinds of walks.

In big cities, you often see dog owners who have allowed their dogs to get the upper hand. Instead of exercising, they stop every few feet, whenever the dog feels the urge. It's not an enjoyable way to proceed. You'll be glad you trained him that there is a difference between *his* walks and your walks.

If you want to advance his training, it's a good idea to sign up for an obedience class. Some trainers offer a "Puppy Kindergarten" class. In basic obedience, he'll learn to obey the commands even with the distraction of other dogs and people. Griffons are very clever and are often the stars of these classes. You may get the urge to train on to competition, and compete for an obedience title.

Activities and Events

Brussels Griffons are fun to show in the breed ring, smart and confident in the AKC's Obedience and Rally events, and competitive in Agility. They make wonderful therapy dogs, delighting patients and charming caregivers. Griffs enjoy taking up a dog sport or pursuing an activity as much as their owners do.

Training your dog for either Obedience or Rally can be fun for both you (or your dog's handler) and the Griff. It's special time spent together that can forge a stronger bond between the two. Additionally, the skills learned for the Novice level in such competitions can serve as an excellent foundation for Agility training and therapy work. The training can also help your dog pass the Canine Good Citizen test.

These activities are appropriate for Brussels Griffons of all ages; even seniors can benefit from learning new skills, keeping them mentally and physically active.

Dog Shows

Dog shows were invented so that breed experts could select the best specimens, giving guidance to breeders as to which dogs they should use to perpetuate the breed and which ones they shouldn't.

That is the theory behind dog shows. But it was never the reality. People participate in such shows because they love dogs, and because showing is a fun way to spend time with their dog.

Knowledgeable breeders don't need the opinion of a judge in order to evaluate their breeding

Champion Toobee's Rembrandt won Best of Breed at the Westminster dog show in 1999.

stock; they should know which faults are major and which are minor. Breeders show because they want to see how their dogs measure up against other people's dogs. Exhibitors show because it gives them a chance to be around like-minded people, people who are devoted to dogs and like to talk endlessly about them.

There are numerous clubs you can join if you are interested in spending even more time talking about dogs and doing things with them, including your local kennel club. Five thousand of such organizations are members of the American Kennel Club. Go to the AKC Web site to find the club in your area.

Because Brussels Griffons are fairly rare, they don't always appear at every dog show. When they do, entries tend to be small, usually from three to ten Griffs. The one place where there are always Griffons is at their National Specialty show, held every year in Louisville, Kentucky, in mid-March. At that show more than a hundred

What to Take to a Dog Show
- Folding chair
- Shade umbrella
- Exercise pen; for Griffs, 36-inch (91.4-cm) size is best
- Water bowl
- Food dish
- Plastic bags to clean up after your dog
- Grooming towel
- Treats, such as liver or hot dog
- Show lead
- Longer lead for walking
- Lunch, snacks, and drinks for yourself!

Griffs are exhibited. Breeders and exhibitors from all over the country and the world attend. After the Specialty show there are four all-breed events at the Kentucky Fair and Exposition Center in Louisville, each with an entry of around a hundred Griffs. Many of these dogs are already champions, so the Best of Breed class is a wonderful place to observe the most outstanding Brussels Griffons of the year. These events have entries of more than four thousand dogs of all breeds every day and are among the largest dog shows in the country.

Another venue with a large entry of Brussels Griffons is the annual Westminster Kennel Club dog show in New York City, which takes place in February. The Top 5 show-winning champions in each breed are invited, and only champions

The dog show judge checks the Brussels Griffon's conformation.

How Does a Dog Become a Champion?

A dog must win a total of 15 points from at least three different judges. Included in these points must be at least two major wins under different judges. A major is a win of 3, 4, or 5 points. The number of dogs in the competition determines the number of points awarded.

The point schedule varies for different regions of the country, depending on the average number of Brussels Griffons being shown in a given region. The AKC changes the point schedules annually and always spells them out in the show catalog.

are allowed to enter. There are usually 12 to 30 champion Brussels Griffons at this show.

The American Brussels Griffon Association holds a Roving Specialty show every fall, in a different location each year. The details are spelled out on the organization's Web site.

To find out where dog shows are being held, check the events calendar of the *AKC Gazette*, or at *www.infodog.com*, or at the Web site of any of the dog show superintendents.

How do dog shows work? A dog show is basically an elimination contest. Winning dogs go on to the next level until they are defeated. The last undefeated dog at the day's end is Best in Show.

There are six regular classes, divided by sex and age. At a specialty, the Open and Bred-by-Exhibitor classes for Brussels Griffons are further divided by coat type, rough and smooth.

• **Puppy class:** Dogs at least six months old and under a year. At large shows and specialties, this class is further divided for puppies under nine months and over nine months of age.

• **Twelve to eighteen months:** Dogs in this age range that are not yet champions.

• **Novice:** Dogs that have never won a blue ribbon in any higher class, have won no more than three first prizes in this class, and have never gone on to the Winners or Reserve categories.

• **Bred by exhibitor:** Dogs bred and owned by the handler or a member of his or her immediate family.

• **American bred:** Dogs born in the United States as a result of a mating that took place in the United States. This class is an anachronism from the early days of dog shows, when many of the winning dogs were imported from other countries.

• **Open:** All dogs of any age or country of birth, including champions, may be shown in Open.

A sturdy toy dog with a thickset, well-balanced body.

The winners of each class come back and compete for Winners. Once all males and all females have been judged, champions enter the ring to compete for Best of Breed, also referred to as Specials class.

Canine Good Citizen

This program puts your dog through her paces to see if she is properly socialized. Your dog must be able to perform a series of ten exercises that can be learned as part of basic obedience training. The main thrust of the test is to show that your Brussels Griffon is even-tempered, well-mannered, and friendly, and never aggressive, shy, or fearful. The tests involve following simple commands such as *sit, stay,* and *down,* loose-leash walking exercises, and reactions to distraction and strangers. If she passes, she's completed the first step in becoming a registered therapy dog.

Therapy Dog

Therapy dogs provide comfort and companionship to patients in hospitals, nursing homes, and other locations where the presence of a calm, happy animal would be beneficial. The dog's visits increase emotional well-being, promote healing, and improve the quality of life for the patients.

Brussels Griffons make wonderful therapy dogs. They bring joy to patients with their outgoing nature, friendly attitude, and love of being held and stroked. They bring sparkle to a sterile day, provide a lively subject for conversation, and rekindle old memories of previously owned pets for everyone who meets them.

How about soccer?

Research has proven that four-footed therapists lower patients' blood pressure and relieve stress and depression. The moment a Brussels Griffon prances into a care facility, most people start to smile regardless of how ill they are or how badly they feel, truly benefiting from the unconditional love and acceptance a therapy dog offers. Many patients are unable to keep their own dog and will never experience the joys of dog ownership again. Therapy dogs bring them some of that joy.

To register your Griff as a therapy dog, contact Therapy Dogs International (TDI), a volunteer group organized to provide qualified dogs and handlers to facilities where these animals are needed.

To meet the requirements of this occupation, your Brussels Griffon must pass the AKC's Canine Good Citizen test and then be assessed by a TDI evaluator.

A relatively new program, established by TDI, is Children Reading to Dogs. Teachers discovered that bringing dogs into classrooms and libraries was wonderful for children, particularly those who were struggling to read and embarrassed by their mistakes; they were much more eager to read to dogs than to other people. The calm presence of the dog gave them confidence. Therapy Dog International's reading program is a great opportunity for children to interact with and learn about dogs in a positive manner.

The best medicine: Medical doctors and psychologists are in agreement that dogs are the best medicine for alleviating stress, whether caused by being on the job eight hours a day, interpersonal relationships, caring for a family, or the like. A dog will provide love, affection, and a gentle touch. The responsibility of walking her is great for reducing stress. Stroking a dog has proven to reduce blood pressure and lessen headaches. Having a dog with you has been shown to help remedy feelings of apprehension and nervousness and bring people out of depression. Owning a Brussels Griffon is a wonderful job for an older person who has retired. Brussels Griffons are great at making you feel worthwhile.

Obedience

Obedience is one of the oldest AKC competitions; it was first held in 1936.

The Griffon must demonstrate a variety of skills, requiring teamwork and communication between the dog and handler. The basic objective of obedience trials is to recognize dogs

Anyone for a swim?

I prefer boating.

that have been trained to behave in the home, in public places, and in the presence of other dogs. The dog must demonstrate willingness and enjoyment while doing the exercises, which include:

- On- and off-leash heeling
- Standing for exam
- Maintaining a *Sit* and a *Down* position as commanded with the handler at a distance or out of sight
- Recall
- Dropping on recall
- Retrieving on flat and over a jump
- Directed retrieval
- Scent article discrimination and retrieval

Each Griffon and handler team starts with 200 points divided among the exercises; a score of 170 or better is needed to qualify for this competition. Three qualifying legs are needed for a title. Different exercises are used for each of the three levels, which are Novice, Open, and Utility.

There are also six non-titling classes that can be entered to prepare for the titling ones, or just for fun. They are Pre-Novice, Graduate Novice, Graduate Open, Brace, Veterans, and Versatility.

Rally

Rally is the newest of the AKC events. It is intended to be a bridge between the Canine Good Citizen program and formal Obedience competition. It allows an inexperienced dog and/or handler to gain ring experience without the stress that can occur in the formal Obedience ring.

Rally is a sport in which the dog and handler complete a course that has been designed by the rally judge. The judge tells the handler to begin, and the dog and handler proceed at their own pace through a course of designated stations (ten to twenty, depending on the competition level). Each station has a sign providing instructions of what is to be performed. Scoring is not as rigorous as traditional obedience contests. AKC Rally has 45 potential exercises. Level I classes are done with the dog on leash and include 12 to 15 exercises. Level II classes are done off leash and involve 12 to 18 exercises, including at least one jump. The judge says nothing during the performance, which lasts from the time the dog and handler cross the starting line until they cross the finish line.

Rally Novice is worked on leash; all other classes are off leash. In addition, all classes other than Rally Advanced Excellent are divided into A and B classes. "A" is for dogs that don't have a title in that level, or an Obedience title; "B" is for those who are continuing in the same

Teaching the **Sit** *command.*

Griffons are great at agility.

level after titling or who may have an Obedience title. In Novice, if the handler has put either a Rally or Obedience title on any dog, the team must compete in the "B" class whether or not the dog has a title.

Agility

Agility is the ultimate fun sport for you and your Brussels Griffon. It will create a bond between you and your dog and give her confidence and keep you fit, as such training involves vigorous exercise on your part. It is also one of the most exciting canine sports for spectators. In agility trials, a dog demonstrates her physical versatility by following cues from the handler to work her way through a timed obstacle course, which has jumps, tunnels, weave poles, and other impediments.

Agility competitions began in England in 1978. The AKC held its first agility trial in 1994, and it is now the fastest growing dog sport in the United States.

The AKC offers two types of agility classes. The first is the Standard Class, which includes obstacles such as the dog walk, the A-frame, and seesaw. The second is Jumpers with Weaves, which involves only jumps, tunnels, and weaves poles. Both classes offer increasing levels of difficulty to earn the Novice, Open, Excellent, and Master titles.

After completing both an Excellent Standard title and Excellent Jumpers title, a dog and handler team can compete for the MACH (Master Agility Champion title). Watching these dogs at the top level run through their course is incredibly exciting.

Griffons are emotionally sensitive, but should never be shy or aggressive.

A proper Griffon is muscular, compact, and well-boned.

Books

The Griffon Bruxellois by Doone Raynham. Published by t.f.h. Kingdom Books, England. Copyright 1998. The best book about Brussels Griffons, written by a true breed expert. Information on buying, training, stripping, showing, and breeding Brussels Griffons.

The Brussels Griffon Primer 2nd Edition by Richard A Ball. Published by the National Brussels Griffon Club. Copyright 1998. A 120-page soft-cover book with pictures of rough and smooth Brussels Griffons and 19 chapters on different aspects of the breed. NBGC, c/o Peggy Fischer, 2428 Bellefontaine, Houston, TX 77030-3102.

Carole A. White's Griffon Grooming Guide by Carole A. White. Published by the National Brussels Griffon Club. Copyright 1985. A guide that covers grooming tools, stripping, staging, and rolling coats, for both rough and smooth

coated Griffons. NBGC c/o Peggy Fischer, 2428 Bellefontaine, Houston, TX 77030-3102.

The American Brussels Griffon Association Illustrated Breed Standard Guide Published by the American Brussels Griffon Association. Copyright 2000. A 21 page pictorial booklet prepared by the American Brussels Griffon Association. Using photographs, drawings, and descriptive text, this book explains the American breed standard for the ideal Brussels Griffon.

Brussels Griffon Champions, 2000–2004 (Paperback) by Jan Linzy and Sharae Pata, and *Brussels Griffon Champions, 1991–1999* by Jan Linzy. Both published by Camino Book Inc. P.O. Box 6400, Incline Village, NV 89450. Phone and Fax (775) 831-3078. info@camino-books.com.

Rare Books

Griffon Bruxellois, Griffon Belge, Petit Brabançon by E. Villemot Braun. Revised edition translated to English by Ilda Pucci and Edward McVey. Published by Flaminia Editrice. Copyright: 1989 Revised Edition. This fabulous book contains the best breed history and the most fascinating photos of early Brussels Griffons. For more information e-mail ilgrif@tin.it. This book is fascinating for true Brussels Griffon fans.

The Cult of the Griffon Bruxellois, Second Edition by Mabel Parker-Rhodes. Published by Idle, Bradford, Watmoughs Limited. Copyright: 1931. Pictures of English Griffons, and an American section written by Iris de la Torre Bueno, secretary of the Brussels Griffon Club of America.

A Griff's eyes should be clear and bright.

A clean Griffon is a happy Griffon!

Griffon Bruxellois by Marjorie Cousens. Published by W. and G. Foyle Ltd. Copyright: 1960. This is written by an English breeder, with advice on breeding and rearing the Brussels Griffon. It contains photographs of English Griffons of the day, with valuable historical data on the development of the breed in England.

Toy Dogs How to Breed and Rear Them: Being The Life Of A Griffon Bruxellois by Muriel Handley Spicer. Published by Adam and Charles Black. Copyright 1902. Written by one of the early English breed experts, the book is ". . . a short account of the life of a little dog, and the ailments which, alas! are the heritage of every puppy that is ever born, of whatever breed."

Small Dogs, Big Hearts by Darlene Arden. Published by Howell Book House, 2006. This book details the special needs of toy dogs. A complete guide to the care and training of little dogs.

Video

The Brussels Griffon Video, American Kennel Club. A valuable reference tool for judges, serious fanciers, and breeders. This videotape illustrates the breed standard and shows various coat colors in the rough and smooth variety. Examples of dogs standing for examination and gaiting, and side-by-side comparisons of different dogs. 20 minutes.

Books on Training

Don't Shoot the Dog!: The New Art of Teaching and Training (Paperback) by Karen Pryor. Published by Bantam Books, 1999. The author teaches how to housetrain and put an end to

Brussels Griffons have no concept of size, and often boss around much larger dogs.

undesirable behavior. It's not only a training book, but delves deeply into animal psychology.

How to Be Your Dog's Best Friend by the Monks of New Skete. Published by Little, Brown and Co. Original edition 1978, update 2002. A step-by-step training manual with details to every aspect of dog ownership.

The Art of Raising a Puppy by the Monks of New Skete. Published by Little, Brown and Co., 1991. The book provides detailed information that describe and illustrate the distinctive approach of the Monks, which is a positive method of dog training.

People, Pooches and Problems: Understanding, Controlling and Correcting Problem Behavior in Your Dog by Job Michael Evans. Published by Howell Book House. Evans teaches how to develop your leadership of your dog, as well as how to prevent problems.

Books on Health
How to Buy and Raise a Good Healthy Dog by Terri Shumsky. Published by Doral Publishing, 2001. Lots of easy to understand details regarding your dog's health.

The Angell Memorial Animal Hospital Book of Wellness and Preventive Care for Dogs by

The Brussels Griffon breed has never been numerous or popular. To his fanciers, he is a well-kept secret.

Darlene Arden. Published by McGraw-Hill, June 25, 2004. A calm and sensible book about how to take care of your dog's health, full of useful explanations of technical terms about dog illnesses.

Dog Owner's Home Veterinary Handbook by Delbert G. Carlson, DVM and James M. Giffin, MD. Published by Howell Book House, 1980. This is a good first aid book to have on hand when you have an emergency, or just a question about your dog's health.

Periodicals

Brussels Sprouts. This is a quarterly magazine published by the National Brussels Griffon Club with articles of interest to Brussels Griffon fanciers, including Griffon news, show statistics, photographs, ads, and a breeders' directory composed of members who subscribe to the NBGC Code of Ethics. In order to receive the magazine, you must become a member of the National Brussels Griffon Club. *www.brussels-griffon.net.*

Organizations

National Brussels Griffon Club
www.brussels-griffon.net

American Brussels Griffon Association
www.brussels-griffon.info

Brussels Griffon Forum
www.thebrusselsgriffonforum.org/

Brussels Griffons in Obedience groups.
yahoo.com/group/brusselsgriffonobedience/

Brussels Griffon Rescue Program
www.brusselsgriffonrescue.org/

American Kennel Club
www.akc.org

Therapy Dogs International, Inc.
www.tdi-dog.org

United States Dog Agility Association
www.usdaa.com

Dog show information
www.infodog.com

INDEX

About the Author
Sharon Sakson has been involved with the Brussels Griffon for three decades, during which she's owned and bred twenty champions. She is a journalist in network television news in New York City. She lives in Pennington, New Jersey, with eight Brussels Griffons. She is an AKC judge of Hound and Working breeds, is the author of more than a hundred articles about dogs and canine-related subjects, and is coauthor, with Neil Plakcy, of *Paws and Reflect: Exploring the Bond Between Gay Men and Their Dogs* (Alyson Books, 2006).

Acknowledgments
Many thanks to Dr. Peter Batts of the Trenton Veterinary Hospital, who over the years allowed himself to become an expert on the health of Brussels Griffons. And to excellent Griffon breeders Leila Downen, John Constantine, Leila Downen, Michelle Bracey, and Liz Williams for their continuous support and assistance.

Important Note
This pet owner's manual tells the reader how to buy or adopt, and care for, a Brussels Griffon. The author and publisher consider it important to point out that the advice given in the book is meant primarily for normally developed dogs of excellent physical health and sound temperament.

Anyone who acquires a fully-grown dog should be aware that the animal has already formed its basic impressions of human beings. The new owner should observe the animal carefully, including its behavior toward humans, and, whenever possible, should meet the previous owner.

Caution is further advised in the association of children with dogs, in meeting with other dogs, and in exercising the dog without a leash.

These matters assume even greater importance when the dog is of a Toy breed.

Even well-behaved and carefully supervised dogs can sometimes damage property or cause accidents. It is therefore in the owner's interest to be adequately insured against such eventualities, and we strongly urge all dog owners to purchase a liability policy that also covers their dog.

Photo Credits
Barbara Augello: 46; Norvia Behling: 12 and 25; Kent Dannen: 39, 43, 49, and 82; Tara Darling: 4, 5, 10, 19, 55, 61, 64, 76, 81, 83, and 90; Cheryl Ertelt: 2–3, 8, 9, 14, 21, 26, 27, 28, 29, 31, 32, 33, 34, 35, 36, 37, 38, 44, 47, 50, 51, 54, 62, 65, 66, 67, 68, 69, 72, 75, 77, 78, 79 (top and bottom), 85 (top and bottom), 87, and 91; Isabelle Francais: 13, 16, 18, 40, 41, 42, 45, 73, 84, 88, 89, and 92; Connie Summers: 15, 24, 57, 58, and 93.

Cover Photos
Cheryl Ertelt: back cover; Isabelle Francais: front cover, inside front cover; Connie Summers: inside back cover.

© Copyright 2007 by Barron's Educational Series, Inc.

All rights reserved.
No part of this book may be reproduced in any form, by photostat, microfilm, xerography, or any other means, or incorporated into any information retrieval system, electronic or mechanical, without the written permission of the copyright owner.

All inquiries should be addressed to:
Barron's Educational Series, Inc.
250 Wireless Boulevard
Hauppauge, NY 11788
www.barronseduc.com

ISBN-13: 978-0-7641-3563-7
ISBN-10: 0-7641-3563-5

Library of Congress Catalog Card No. 2006016418

Library of Congress Cataloging-in-Publication Data
Sakson, Sharon R.
  Brussels griffons : everything about purchase, care, nutrition, behavior, and training / Sharon R. Sakson ; filled with full-color photographs.
    p. cm. — (A complete pet owner's manual)
  Includes index.
  ISBN-13: 978-0-7641-3563-7
  ISBN-10: 0-7641-3563-5
  1. Brussels griffon. I. Title. II. Series.

SF429.B79S25 2007
636.76—dc22   2006016418

Printed in China
9 8 7 6 5 4 3 2 1